# INSIDIOUS CHANGES:

# A Short History of Big Government and the Resulting Crisis

**Dean A. Dohrman, Ph.D.**

**3** CORNERS BOOKS

ISBN: 979-8-648-61930-2

www.politicalfaqs.com

# TABLE OF CONTENTS

# I. THE PROBLEM

*"A child educated only at school is an uneducated child."*
*~ George Santayana*

Get your health care here! Get your free education here! Get your housing here! Get your food stamps here! Get your pension here! Get your universal income here! Get your (fill in the blank) here!

It seems that politicians have little problem promising the moon in their campaigns, but the challenge comes with the delivery. So, why do they continue? Because we allow it, and as a result, every American owes in excess of $72,340: that is every American, from infancy until taking on room temperature. The bad news is it only gets worse. Our national debt that equated to 53.19 percent of our national income (measured as Gross Domestic Product, all goods and services produced during a year) in 1960, fell to 34.52 percent in 1980, but rose again to 58.97 percent in 2000. Well, historically not too bad, you might think, but the is reality there has been an explosion of expenditures since that time. However, just before the COVID-19 scare our federal government's spending spree amounts to over $23 trillion (that's $23,000,000,000,000,000!) with a debt/GDP ratio of 107.09 percent! "Well," some respond, "we obviously need to cut back on military spending." That won't cut it either as the military spending of $700 billion annually pales in comparison to Medicare/Medicaid expenditures of $1.3 trillion and social/income security expenses of another $1.3 trillion.[1] Oh, and let's not even get into all the debt and unfunded pensions in state and local governments! Add to that all the spending involved in the COVID-19 response, and the numbers grow ever larger. How in the world did we get in this mess? We got here by expecting unrealistic results from our government and institutions, and then having those expectations set the price for all of us.

To put it in another context, ask yourself this question: Would you purposely put diesel in your gasoline engine vehicle? I would hope not. What if you unknowingly put diesel in your gasoline engine? Of course, you would have the same outcome whether you knowingly or

---

[1] US National Debt Clock, retrieved from www.usdebtclockorg.

unknowingly put the wrong fuel in your tank, eventually, the engine will falter. Unfortunately, this metaphor is very relevant to our constitutional government today. Knowingly and unknowingly, Americans, elected and unelected leaders, are damaging the institutions of self-government that have served us well for over two centuries. How? By raising unrealistic expectations for government, and frankly, pricing the middle class out of existence. One of the oldest tricks in the book for a government is to debase their currency so that debt can be repaid more cheaply. So, every year your dollars are worth a little bit less, a camouflaged way for you to subsidize government spending. What can we do to counteract this long-term damage? First and foremost, all of us should be involved in and informed of our system of self-government so that we can hold our elected officials accountable and make wise choices at the ballot box. In human history, it is a rare gift that we have inherited, but much too often we take it for granted. On the other hand, we should not be too hard on ourselves. Genuine appreciation is difficult if we do not understand what we have inherited, and conversely, what we have lost. Unfortunately, this inheritance is often ignored or obscured, but this book is intended to counter such educational shortcomings concerning our past.

Before I go any further, let me explain what I mean by the title, *Insidious Changes*. Shortly after the American centennial, a political movement became prominent that changed the very nature of the United States. The Progressives took a framework of government designed to be small, limited, and difficult to change morphing it into a "living document" that could be changed by a few activists rather than a majority of Americans. The ensuing activists did not pursue an outright, open revolution; they used a much more Fabian approach.[2]

---

[2] In 1884, a group of British intellectuals formed a group to pursue democratic socialism in a gradual, reformist (rather than revolutionary) manner. They adopted the name Fabian Society in honor of the Roman general Fabius the Delayer who avoided direct confrontation with Hannibal in favor of short skirmishes in an effort to win by gradually weakening the opposing force. The Society had a significant influence on the formation and rise of the Labour Party in the early 20th Century. Several famous Britons belonged to the Society including Sidney and Beatrice Webb, H. G. Wells, George Bernard Shaw, Emmeline Pankhurst, Bertrand Russell for a short time, Clement Attlee, and Tony Blair. The Fabian Society ideals spread to other parts of the British Empire and they founded the London School of Economics and Political Science in 1895.

~ 2 ~

They masked their changes, usually only a few at a time, pointing to expanding definitions within the Constitution, technological changes, and societal needs. However, behind every change, a concentration of federal power accompanied the new interpretations and policies. These challenges to the original constitutional arrangement came from two primary sources, the activist presidency, and an activist judiciary. Only occasionally did the reformers involve the states in changing the complexion of the Constitution using the amendment process. Throughout the process, the constitutional shift of power to the federal government subtly continued for nearly a century before being successfully challenged. The size of government got out of hand as did the spending. The pie of government benefits continually expands as many Americans just whistle by the graveyard. This challenge to our constitutionally limited government has developed into a standoff that pits an electorate against itself.

This book is an attempt to elucidate our constitutional system, how it started, why it includes specific provisions, and how these provisions have been subject to interpretation and action over the years. Unfortunately, many of these changes have led us to political dysfunction because of the very nature of the changes. The Progressive changes have led to problems because the ever-expanding authority of the federal government is constructed on top of a constitutional framework designed for limited government. Because so much of this has occurred little by little over time, it seems that we reached a crisis point overnight. However, the fact is that changes crept in over decades, and these changes cannot be addressed without a long-term effort.

The national debt statistics shared above have resulted from years of politicians promising that the government can solve every problem. Of course, it is impossible to find perfection in an imperfect world, but the easy answer is to throw money at problems. Public education does not return the results we need and expect? Throw money at the problem! There are people living in poverty? Throw money at them, and that will solve all their problems! The economy is in severe adjustment because of globalization? Throw money into the system, and everyone will feel better! If that doesn't work, give them cheap interest and they will feel richer! No amount of money addresses the real problem in these examples, but politicians can say they are doing

Insidious Changes

something for you. Yes, they are, they are putting diesel in the tank of your gasoline engine.

I use the metaphor of an engine to illustrate the thesis of the book. It is true, a car with a gasoline engine can run with a small amount of diesel in the fuel tank, but a steadily increasing diet will eventually cause it to falter. Our problem is as simple as diesel engines are made for diesel and gasoline engines are made for gasoline. The crisis of our time is that so many generations have been taught to use diesel in our gasoline engine, that many are married to this incorrect notion and will not modify their behavior to salvage the engine. Education and sharing are the keys to restoring the foundational rules that held a vast nation together and made it a bastion of hope for the world. "A light upon a hill," as Ronald Reagan so eloquently restated many times. However, the time for action is now because this great light is fading.

The Annenberg Public Policy Center conducts an annual survey of American civic knowledge, a reflection of our next generation's educational background. In the 2019 study, only 39 percent of those surveyed could name the three branches of government. Think about that, only 39 percent, not even close to a majority, could correctly answer one of the most fundamental questions concerning our government.[3] Unfortunately, this lack of being informed leads to acceptance of changes that act as poison within our system and threaten the institutions that are designed to preserve freedom. I became involved in a severe example of this threat presented by a lack of fundamental knowledge as a state representative: a basic principle that protects every American from arbitrary loss.

I will illustrate my point by referring back to the old Soviet Union. In this communist dictatorship, Josef Stalin chose his enemies by the millions, and many just disappeared into the night, never to be seen again. However, those of higher public stature usually received a "show trial" set out for an explanation of how the person ran afoul of the supreme forces that be, and to warn others not to follow in such a path. Unfortunately, on today's college campuses, we have a similar style of oppressive prosecution.

---

[3] The Annenberg Public Policy Center, retrieved from https://www.annenbergpublicpolicycenter.org/americans-civics-knowledge-increases-2019-survey/.

For years now, administrators have shown young students the door out of higher education with hardly an explanation of why. Basic American principles like due process (understanding the charge presented, being able to respond to the charge, presenting evidence in your favor, etc.) have been swept out the door all because of a letter issued nearly a decade ago.

Title IX became an issue because of a Dear Colleague letter produced by the Obama administration in 2011. The document targeted investigations on sexual assault claims made on college campuses and threatened ominous consequences if results could not be demonstrated sooner rather than later. As a result, the system became streamlined, often with the removal of due process from these proceedings. In case you are unfamiliar with this process, let me quickly summarize: many Title IX proceedings mirror the kings' old Star Chamber in that the accused will be called in without prior notification of the charge (or very little), no specific allegation will be written, the accuser will not appear, there is no cross-examination, and no opposing legal counsel is allowed to be present if any type of cross-examination does occur. These practices are certainly in violation of the bedrock principle of due process, a long-standing constitutional provision in America which we inherited from England (the English Parliament outlawed the Star Chamber in 1641). Unfortunately, time continues to pass and no rights have been restored on campus. All these are basic constitutional violations that are occurring in an administrative state sold to us as designed to protect and help us!

Central to individual protection under federal law in the Bill of Rights is the 5th Amendment and its provision of due process. The right to face your accuser, to be presented with the evidence against you, the right of appeal, and most importantly, the presumption of innocence until proven guilty are embodied in this constitutional concept. In fact, past generations were so supportive of this principle of due process they repeated it in the 14th Amendment to make certain that individual states upheld this fundamental tenet. However, something happened under the Obama administration that has threatened this bedrock of the American legal system.

Proponents of the Obama provisions argued that these measures are necessary to achieve justice in sexual assault and harassment cases. To have the accuser subject to cross-examination would be too

Insidious Changes

traumatic, so the defendant has no clear idea of who is accusing, what the accusation is, or even when it occurred, let alone have the ability to defend him/herself. Often they are given the "opportunity" to leave school without further action. The problem here is trying to re-enter school elsewhere, which puts a damper on trying to ignite a career. Add to that the cost to go to court and fight the allegation, which starts in the neighborhood of $250,000. Talk about a student debt problem!

At least US Education Secretary Betsy DeVos acknowledged the problem with proposed changes to right these wrongs of the Obama-era proceedings, but well into 2020 they have yet to be distributed as the new rules. Another problem with this route is that even if formally adopted, these changes are not permanent. Therefore, down the line, another administration may go back to the Obama administration's policy of due process denial.

Why should due process apply equally to both parties? Because expulsion or suspension, coupled with being accused of sexual misconduct, can destroy a young person's career and carries life-long consequences. For justice to be served, due process must be applied, and not merely exist as an option for the select few. Unfortunately, this basic principle has apparently slipped away from a significant portion of our population.

This lack of understanding involving due process is just one example of our national deficit in basic civics education. Thomas Jefferson put it this way, "If a nation expects to be ignorant and free . . . it expects what never was and never will be." To head off this inevitable outcome is the goal of this book: to present in a readable, enjoyable format, a way to learn the history of constitutional heritage, what the Constitution is and is not.

In the effort to illuminate the past and present, this book traces the experience of small English settlements that grew into 13 colonies, eventually forming a new nation, which expanded across the continent, grew into an enormous economic engine, and eventually became a political and military superpower. Obviously, such an experience would result in pressure to implement governmental changes. Possessing foresight, the Founders relied on the flexibility of federalism to adjust to change while adapting measured changes through the amendment process. However, their system has been

Insidious Changes

successfully used only 27 times in the history of the country, whereas other methods have been heavily utilized.

The Founders of what we know today as the United States of America rebelled against too much authority in a central place, namely a concentration of power within the executive branch of King George III and his parliamentary ministers in London. As a remedy, they sought to mitigate, if not replace, such a concentration of power, and to this end, they swore their lives, their fortunes, and their sacred honor.

After victory, the Founders had no intention of replicating the ruling cadre of London on their side of the Atlantic Ocean. In an attempt to keep a dispersal of power, the Articles of Confederation operated with an executive who derived power from the legislature composed of an equal number of delegates from each state. Every year the Confederation Congress elected a president to implement and enforce their laws. In turn, the Confederation Congress operated within strict limitations, and as a result, could only petition the states for revenue, could not regulate interstate commerce, and remained constrained with many other tight restrictions. The result became an ineffective government and frustration that boiled to such a point that the Founders called for decisive change. However, before instituting wholesale changes, they reflected carefully on the history of constitutional government.

In the Early Modern period, the decentralized system of feudal lords gave way to the political trend of the centralized monarchy. This model reached its apex in the reign of Louis XIV in France. These monarchies drove the formation of nation-states (people of like background forming into political unions), but no political order goes without challenges, and so it proved to be with centralized monarchies.

In England, as the middle class rose and sought influence, they pointed back to the precedent of the *Magna Carta*[4] as evidence of limited kingly authority. Of course, the Stuart kings in England pushed back on the rising middle class within the House of

---

[4] In 1215, the English barons forced King John to sign the Magna Carta acknowledging rights to their inheritance. This is often considered the beginning point in English history of the rule of law: no one, including the king, would be considered above the law.

Commons, but in the end, they could not prevail. War ensued, but the political trappings such as the monarchy and Parliament survived, although significantly changed in the end. The justification for usurping the power of the king came in the form of a cry for individual liberty. The English colonists picked up this philosophy and took individual liberty to a structure of self-government that would impact global history: a nation based on an idea of liberty rather than merely raw power.

One principle that has not changed, no matter what type of governing structure, is that being a viable state involves physical security and stability for everyday lives of citizens. Such protection includes private property rights so that people can build their financial security (Fourth and Eighth Amendments), as well as the rule of law providing individual legal rights, such as the freedom of political expression (First Amendment), protection from arbitrary search and seizure (Fourth Amendment, Fifth Amendment, and Eighth Amendment), and the right to self-protection (the Second Amendment). These cover the basic need for security.[5] However, this also includes the tension of security vs. liberty. Within the American system, this has been expressed from the establishment of our current constitutional system through two of its authors, James Madison and Alexander Hamilton.

In 1775, the American colonists began a journey to liberty that would become a formalized war the following year. They guarded their new system of liberty to such an extent that they would only organize a loose confederation, eventually codified in the Articles of Confederation fully ratified in 1781. However, this loose confederation pitted the new states often more in rivalry rather than cooperation. By 1787 the newly formed US faced a crisis: external threats existed, as they always do, and the Articles of Confederation could not provide a steady income to support a common defense. Also, and most critical at the moment, financial stability proved elusive to the newly formed confederation. Hamilton viewed the solution of security and stability in the context of the nation. Madison viewed both on a smaller scale, always at least somewhat

---

[5] Abraham Maslow's hierarchy of needs basically argues that fundamental human needs, such as food, water, and safety, must be met before person can achieve higher levels of accomplishment.

Insidious Changes

apprehensive of a government too far removed from the people (Thomas Jefferson would develop this philosophy even further). In the end, they agreed to a new form of government that sought to unify the nation, retain the dispersion of power, and in the end, preserve individual liberty. The preservation of liberty would be through structural safeguards that the British form of government did not, and could not, provide. So, in a conscious effort to eliminate the problems associated with the parliamentary concentration of power while avoiding the pitfalls of confederation, the Americans formed a new and unique governmental system, federalism.

Often the terms national and federal are used interchangeably, but this is incorrect. A federal form of government, federalism, is a political system in which there are concurrent units of government; these governments have specific authority, and the existence of each entity is protected. We do not have a national government as operates in Britain, other European countries, or other regions of the world. However, we do have a unifying force, the supremacy clause[6], and this is all by design of the Founders.

Madison, the primary author of the Constitution, outlined a federal form of government that placed a system of checks and balances within a separation of powers. This fundamental principle is a fact taught in every introductory American government class that has ever existed. However, we are often not informed that this system goes beyond the three branches of legislative, executive, and judicial. It also includes the states. The states have the most authority under the Constitution, and they have mechanisms to overcome unwieldy federal power. This feature would keep nationalists, such as Hamilton, in check. Hamilton should not be perceived as a negative force; in fact, some nationalism was undoubtedly needed to pull the states together. However, the prospect of too much nationalism caused great angst among the Founders for fear that the British experience would be revived and liberty would be lost again. Instead, states would retain significant power and keep government close to the people who would serve as watchdogs over government. Even today, after years of eroding power for the states, most of us live our

---

[6] The supremacy clause is found in Article VI of the US Constitution designates federal law as the supreme law of the land. Therefore, if state constitutions or statutes are in conflict with federal provisions, the federal prevails.

Insidious Changes

daily lives directly subject to numerous state statutes (various licenses, taxes, professional regulation, etc.).

It is somewhat difficult for us, now so far removed from that historic event during the summer of 1787, to comprehend how vital the states were to the system. This importance persisted for years: think back to the Civil War and its circumstances. Robert E. Lee, an American, became the military leader of the Confederate forces. Again, hard for us to imagine an American fighting other Americans! We can't truly comprehend because we think differently than the famous general. Lee fought to defend Virginia, his home. Today, we certainly identify with our state, but mostly we identify ourselves as Americans: America first, so to speak. For Lee, it was Virginia first: he lived out his inherited understanding of the Constitution as a collection of states, and as a Virginian, he defended his homeland.

In the colonial period, there was no United States. There was New York, Pennsylvania, New Jersey, Massachusetts, etc., but no United States. Their loyalties were with the king and his politics, trade, as well as other vital elements that all ran back to London. It was not until Parliament "leaned" on the colonies for money that they began to find common ground for unification. Benjamin Franklin's Albany Plan failed in the 1750s, but the Stamp Act Congress quickly took root a decade later. Motivation (albeit negative motivation) stimulated the colonies to cohesive action.

The debate over the Constitution brought forward the old colonial divisions. Political leaders did not trust giving authority to another entity: Virginians should rule Virginians! This persisted throughout the first half of the 19th Century, and after the Civil War the South continued to resist Northern influence by flexing their state authority.

The 10th Amendment reserves power to the states, and this remained the "right way" of government for many Americans for many years. In fact, during the early part of the republic, the states unquestionably exerted the most influence over daily life. If you had been born on a Missouri farm in 1869, you would have little contact with the federal government. You had no reason to take a very difficult trip to Washington, DC. You probably could not have gotten away from the farm work to take the long journey if you had a reason to travel east. Other than the post office, the federal government had very few agency offices in the countryside, so the federal government

Insidious Changes

existed as some distant entity that meant little to your daily life (there wasn't even an income tax at the time!).

The state, on the other hand, had a presence in every county, the county court house, so the state government was real to the daily lives of citizens. They paid property tax to the county, recorded deeds at the county courthouse, and the state capitol could be reached without traveling across country. So, even after the Civil War, the state predominated in domestic politics. However, technology, specifically railroads, began to change this arrangement.

The federal government began to regulate the rails in the latter part of the 19th Century. Life began to move a little faster as we approached the 20th Century. Income tax came with the 16th Amendment, and the federal government was in your pocket! (Probably not at first as it started with just the very wealthy, but it soon moved into everybody's purse.) With the advent of the automobile, the federal government started building highways. The "feds" crept into every aspect of life. The federal government began to do such things as inspect our meat and other food as well as drugs. Through the 14th Amendment the federal government began to enforce its laws, so two governments, federal and state, placed constraints on daily activity. The regular police powers of the state (health, safety, and welfare) and an assorted bag of federal rules, regulations, and programs all influenced daily life. In the 1930s, the New Deal placed money in the pockets of ordinary citizens: the Civilian Conservation Corps hired young men to plant trees, the original Agricultural Adjustment Act paid farmers money not to farm (until the Supreme Court forced a change and they began receiving payments for conservation methods), and the Works Progress Administration provided money for public projects. The federal government was everywhere!

The concept of federalism has changed dramatically not only from technological necessities, but also from events: Supreme Court decisions, Congressional action, and funding policies. As a result, there are three broadly defined eras of federalism in American history: dual (or layer cake) federalism (1787-1933), cooperative (or marble cake) federalism (1933-1968), and new federalism (1969-Present). As a result, it is difficult for us today to distinguish between the governmental entities that exercise authority over our lives. To grasp these distinctions, we need to carefully review these historical

~ 11 ~

eras, as well as the molders of federalism: specifically activist presidents and high court justices.

Dual federalism is the traditional theory of federalism based on the Constitution. If the elastic clause (Article I) is set aside for a moment, areas of federal and state governments are quite clear (powers of Congress are listed in the Constitution, while other powers are reserved to the states through the 10th Amendment). In dual federalism, the division of powers became:

- Federal: declare war; coin of money; regulate immigration; enter treaties; appoint foreign ambassadors; regulate interstate commerce
- States: health; education; exercise of police powers; regulation of marriage; voting
- Shared: taxation; creation of courts; laws for the general welfare

As seems inevitable, tension existed and became fully developed with the notion of nullification with the Virginia and Kentucky Resolutions, in which states contended that unconstitutional federal statutes could be overruled by the states. However, the Supreme Court helped to establish some early ground rules of federalism. In *McCulloch v. Maryland* (1819), the Court upheld the use of the elastic clause ("Let the end be legitimate . . . and all means . . . consistent with the letter and spirit of the Constitution, are constitutional.") to establish the Bank of the United States.

McCulloch of the Baltimore branch would not pay a tax levied by Maryland. The Court decided that although the bank had no mention in the Constitution, the management of funds is, the bank was "necessary and proper" to conduct this business. Furthermore, the federal government was established by the people not the states, and its authority was sovereign to that of the states (a careful distinction from the Articles of Confederation). In *Gibbons v. Ogden* (1824), the Court ruled that Congressional control of interstate commerce could be "exercised to its utmost extent." Although largely ignored throughout the 19th Century, this principle would be used in the 20th Century to enforce minimum wage law, regulate working conditions, enforce civil rights, etc. As a growing power, and the proliferation of global war, the president has been granted extensive power as commander-in-chief, and what Congress has failed to hand over, they have often surrendered. Today, the legislature fights almost constantly with the executive branch, and policies and actions seem to be on fast tracks to the Supreme Court. In fact, this has become a default remedy for states as it is remains among the few powers left to them when seeking relief from unwanted federal policies and acts, but the system remains more unbalanced than balanced today.

In the system of federalism, checks and balances are intertwined and designed to work together, one being more prominent than the other depending on the situation. The system has become unbalanced over time in several ways: presidential power has dramatically increased, states have lost much of their power, and the Supreme Court has taken on a decisive role in public policymaking. However, the president is still checked by Congress and the Supreme Court. Congress checks itself with two houses, and is subject of Supreme Court decisions. As we will see, the Court does not have an effective check and laid the groundwork for an expansion of its power through judicial review. The check of the state deteriorated during the 20th Century as the Supreme Court incrementally reduced their power through the 14th Amendment. Add to this mix that government has moved further and further away from "We the People" and moved more and more toward rigid bureaucracies that often hide their motivations, including motivations to increase their circle of influence and control.

How did we get here? At this point in time, is there any correction to this path of deteriorating freedom? These are fundamental issues of our time and it is time to address these in a straight-forward manner.

The Founders had a design in mind, a very mechanical design that worked when in balance. Understanding that the nature of humanity is to gather more advantages for selfish purposes, the Founders sought to balance the various forces of the political body in an attempt to keep any singular interest from tipping the scale entirely away from the people. They developed a system based on practical theory and proven practice.

There are constitutional scholars who look at what is and ignore how we got here. If you have ever constructed a house, you know that the foundation, frame, roof, and windows go up rather quickly. This beginning, as important as it is, can hardly be considered a completed project. No one would consider this a perfect structure before insulation, wiring, plumbing, and all the floors and trim are complete. This interior finish is the most time-consuming portion of the project. So, I might suggest, we can look at the US through this analogy of the house; the Founders framed up a constitution that allowed an expansion of civil liberties over the years. If the Founders of this country had not made that first step in declaring equality in the world, how would the rest of the house of freedom ever have been completed? There would have been no structure to build on if they had not made that first step.

Eric Foner asserts that Abraham Lincoln gave our country its second start, but did he push restart, or did he further the mission of the Founders? The second answer is certainly an idea Lincoln expressed. The expansion of the vote during the Jacksonian period, women's suffrage, and the Second Civil Rights era in the 20th Century can be seen as furthering the promise first articulated and acted upon by the Founders. They did not have time to complete the journey, but they started the journey.

Reflection, I believe, can be very illuminating, especially in the realm of problem-solving. Self-governing, as is the case with all aspects of this life, always has its associated problems. Constitutional scholars tend to misrepresent or dismiss the development of American government over the early years of American history and move quickly to the Progressive format that began in the late 19th Century and came of age during the New Deal, reaching its peak with the Great Society. This approach overlooks some critical points of the fundamental grounding and philosophy of governance in the US. This short work is provided to help correct this bias. Hopefully, it is a manageable history of our system of government. It should invoke reflection on changes that have been made, how those changes transformed our system, and what additional changes in the future might do to transform further, or recover, our "Government by the people, for the people, and of the people." Rather than throwing away the blueprint of the Founders, perhaps we should consider what they did correctly, how they constructed a system that has endured, and what we might achieve if we also work within this system.

# II: ESTABLISHING ENGLISH AMERICA

## THE ENGLISH INHERITANCE IN NORTH AMERICA

*The beginning of the US as a country and its constitutional system of governing has its roots in the European Reformation. The German monk Martin Luther (d. 1546) challenged Pope Leo X on several issues in 1517, resulting in the 95 Theses attached to the church door at Wittenberg and launching the modern Christian reform movement we know as the Reformation. This movement would permanently change Europe, as well as England. It began the modern process of the individual being pitted against institutions. These religious changes became intertwined with the rise of the middle class and the idea of limited government.*

*As personal wealth grew and religious understanding took a new turn, the older Church of Rome faced challenges it could not successfully address. These powerful social factors combined and became a trademark of early modern Europe and an ideological perspective in the struggle for political control. The political and religious turmoil bubbled over in England with civil war (1642-51), and the Glorious Revolution (1688) that would firmly place the middle class, represented in the House of Commons, in control of the island country. John Locke would articulate a new philosophy of governing in his* Two Treatises on Government: *a publication that became a beacon for self-government as American colonists became dissatisfied with British rule in the late 18th Century.*

Time travel has fascinated imaginative people for many, many years. H. G. Wells wrote this into a dramatic novel in the 19th Century. He dwelled on the issue of what the future might look like, but in the 20th Century, Irwin Allen took time travel in another direction. His 1966-7 television series "Time Tunnel" whisked Dr. Tony Newman and project director Doug Phillips through time, and found them often "fixing" historical events, putting everything in its right place before moving on to the next (usually historical) event. This premise proved to be an entertaining hour every week and most likely piqued some interest in historical events for some of the viewers. If we could slightly change this scenario, I will attempt to place us in shoes of our ancestors. Wouldn't it be fun if we could travel back in time as an observer, to learn, to really learn how history unfolded? Most likely, this would greatly enlighten our understanding of the present.

If we travel back to England in the 1620s, we find a changing country. The market economy, what we call capitalism, is beginning to grow substantially and open doors of opportunity for more English citizens than ever before. Religion is under transformation as Protestantism is challenging the centuries of orthodoxy handed down from the Vatican. If we are more inclined to Protestant change than approved by the Crown, we might find ourselves under social restrictions, and our deeply held convictions suppressed by outside forces. As a result, we might consider moving to new habitats to live as we chose to live, and that could likely move us to New England.

In the new land, we find that we face many challenges. The wilderness surrounds us with dense forest, wild animals, and natives that can be friendly or hostile. We are concerned about feeding ourselves and find the vast resources of the wilderness very useful in this endeavor. We have many religious friends, and we most likely see them almost daily and certainly in church on Sunday. Most of our time is consumed in survival, and usually, we cooperate with our neighbors rather than fight, but occasionally conflicts arise. If this occurs, we have laws and courts to enforce the laws. These are English laws because we are English citizens, and this fundamental governmental institution, along with our religion, and our undeniable need to cooperate for survival, tends to bond us together in our daily existence. This scenario sums up the most significant portion of our existence. Life was not easy for anyone in New England, but common goals serve as a strong bond. How did all this unfold, you might ask; certainly, we skipped over some important historical details, correct? Correct, we need to go back at least a century further to place all of this in context.

On Halloween, 1517, a little known monk at the time, Martin Luther, went to the doors of All Saints' Church in Wittenberg, Germany, and nailed up 95 Theses (statements) he wished to debate with church authorities. The sale of indulgences had provoked this action (tickets out of Purgatory, if you will) to help raise funds for the building of St. Peter's Basilica in Rome. How in the world, Luther asked himself, could a soul be bought out of a spiritual state that a

Insidious Changes

person's actions had ordained as their fate? This question haunted Luther for some time until he reached a conclusion from the Bible that satisfied his inquiry: only God can forgive sin, not the pope or his representatives. God provides salvation for every individual, and every individual must study the scriptures to find the teachings of God that would eventually free their souls from eternal damnation. Today, a Lutheran will tell you that we are all "justified by faith, through grace." God came to us, we cannot discover Him no matter how insightful and wise we might be, and the revelation God gave to us is contained in the Bible. Read the Holy Scriptures and learn, Luther would advise us, and this had a very significant impact on society.

Suddenly, literacy mattered to every human being. If you could not read the Bible, you could not find God and his salvation provided through Jesus Christ. To help his fellow Germans, Luther translated the Bible into German for all to read. What heresy, the Roman Church proclaimed! The pope, designated by Christ through Peter, held the keys to heaven and hell. No one found salvation without the True Church and participation in its Sacraments. These unfortunate victims in Germany had to be saved from eternal damnation by destroying Luther and his ludicrous ideas. However, Luther could intellectually defend his beliefs, and the Elector of Saxony physically protected him. All this connected to Johann Guttenberg's recent improvements in printing, and Luther's ideas spread quickly through Northern Europe: now, the pope had a real struggle on his hands! As part of the north, Lutheranism entered England and Scotland, and at first, English King Henry VIII (d. 1547) resisted the movement. However, this changed when he ran afoul of Pope Clement VII when he sought a divorce from Catherine of Aragon.

Henry's desire to produce a male heir for the throne that his family had fought so hard to win during the Wars of the Roses (1455-1487) drove him to desperate measures. The remedy ultimately came in the Act of Supremacy in 1534. This legislative act, passed by Parliament, proclaimed the Church of England as unique and the king to be the head of the English institution: a definite break from papal authority. This event set the stage in the early 16th Century as the Tudors moved forward the idea of an English national identity while centralizing their power. Eventually, this centralization of power allowed England to challenge the leading colonial nations of the time, Spain and

Insidious Changes

France, both with more centralized governments than England. This centralization trend proved efficient at mustering resources for war, something they indulged in for centuries. However, several years passed before England became a serious colonial contender.

When Henry's daughter Elizabeth I finally ascended to the throne (1558), England had resolved some internal issues and truly challenged for supremacy on the seas. However, they lacked land colonies, a situation that would change in the 17th Century under the Tudors' Scottish cousins. Elizabeth's Scottish cousin James Stuart ascended to the English throne upon her death in 1603. Under James I, England established its first permanent settlement in North America, Jamestown, Virginia (1607). From this precarious beginning, the colony would eventually discover tobacco. The resulting fad that took off in Europe provided cash sales to colonial farmers giving birth to American commercial agriculture (farming a surplus to sell as opposed to subsistence farming, i.e., farming to survive). However, just as England's global status rose, troubles began to brew at home.

James believed in the divine right of kings: he had been chosen by God (through bloodline) as the ruler of the British people. In his mind, Parliament could not challenge his authority or question his judgment, for God had chosen him to be king! Parliament had a very different idea, however.

During this time of growing capitalism, economic power had shifted from the House of Lords to the House of Commons, the chamber filled with the new and rising middle class that prospered from such activities as the tobacco trade. Then and now, those with money like to have a voice in government, and Parliament had to approve tax increases often paid by the new middle class. Here came the rub for James: he did not believe that Parliament had the right to tell him what to do, but they controlled many sources of money. James managed the situation, but his son Charles I had trouble navigating these rough financial waters (the Stuarts, like most European kings of the time, were involved in many expensive wars). The authoritarian and Catholic inclinations of Charles led to many Puritans, those who wished to cleanse Christianity of the papacy, to move to New England in the Great Migration (which coincides with our time machine move). This continual bickering with Charles produced one of the pillars of English constitutionalism. In May

~ 18 ~

1628, Sir Edward Coke drafted the Petition of Right limiting the monarch's powers of taxation, securing civil rights such as *habeas corpus* (evidence must be produced by the government to hold a person in custody for an extended period of time), and prohibitions on the quartering of troops and martial law.

The Petition of Right passed in Parliament, both Commons and Lords, forcing a reluctant Charles to ratify the measure. The law reinforced the perception of inherited rights as Englishmen, an idea historically embodied in the *Magna Carta*, the first statement of rights signed by King John I in 1215.[7] The power struggle that became the English Civil War changed the power structure of English politics, its constitution, its political philosophy, and eventually became the intellectual basis for American independence.

In 1642, war erupted between the supporters of King Charles I and Parliament. It was partly a religious struggle (Catholicism vs. Protestantism), partly economic (the hereditary landowners vs. the rising middle class), and partly philosophical (the king had unrestricted rights vs. all Englishmen possessed inherited birth rights). Parliament's rebellion against Charles I resulted in the legislature's rule over England without a king. The beheading of Charles I in 1649 put the iron-fisted Oliver Cromwell in the position of being the executive. When Charles II fled to continental Europe in 1651, the fight ended. Cromwell kept order in Parliament for most of the remaining decade, but after his death, Cromwell's son Robert could not hold the body together. Parliament turned back to the Stuarts and restored Charles II in 1660.

Charles II learned from history: he kept Parliament pacified, and as a result, ruled moderately. However, Charles' brother James II returned to the old family trait of irritating Parliament with his disregard for their opinions. However, as much as opposing philosophies caused friction, the breaking point came with religion.

James II baptized his son a Catholic, which seemed, in effect, a thumbing of his nose at Parliament dominated by Puritans and other Protestants. As a result, they dethroned James and offered the crown

---

[7] In 1215, the English barons forced King John to sign the Magna Carta acknowledging rights to their inheritance. This is often considered the beginning point in English history of the rule of law: no one, including the king, would be considered above the law.

to his daughter Mary. Mary, being married to William of Orange, a powerful Protestant ruler in Europe, settled the issue of religion. Along with the issue of religion, Parliament also established who ruled England: the uncontestable power would reside in Parliament. Parliament even passed a Bill of Rights (protection of their legislative rights) to solidify their constitutional position against the crown. These events are known as the Glorious or Bloodless (although a few people did die) Revolution of 1688. With the struggle for power settled, Parliament needed to explain its action, and so John Locke entered the scene.

John Locke, an English physician and philosopher, wrote *Two Treatises on Government*, published in 1690. In this foundational work of classical liberalism, Locke first argued against the theory of the divine right of kings. With that much said, in the second treatise he moved on to what government should be, a social contract (or compact), and it still influences us to this day.

Locke argued that the purpose of society is to provide security. Otherwise, we would remain in a state of nature where we all have perfect freedom, answerable only to our creator. However, people are people, and sometimes those without will take from those with: therefore, we require a societal compact to ensure personal security. Locke conceded that we all must give up some rights to have a society that preserves our security. However, certain rights cannot be forfeited: these are life, liberty, and property. These can only be denied through due process. The Stuart kings had violated these rights, and as a result, the contract became null and void. In this situation, the citizens had a right to revolt, and so they did. In fact, Algernon Sidney, another influential English republican theorist with his *Discourses Concerning Government* (posthumously published in 1698), became entangled in the Rye House Plot to assassinate both Charles II and James II and suffered execution after conviction. Although James II survived the 1683 plot against his life, he did not survive the rebellion of Parliament. He tried to mount a return to the throne only to be defeated by William of Orange at the Battle of Boyne in 1690, and the new social contract concept, as well as Protestantism, proved to be solidly entrenched.

Despite all this trouble at home, England continued to vie for a position as a global colonial power. The colonists began to learn that they had to provide most of the colonial defense, which they

Insidious Changes

accomplished through local armed militias. These militias typically defended settled areas and were slow to expand. However, after a series of wars in North America, the newly formed United Kingdom of Great Britain and Ireland (combining England, Wales, Scotland, and Ireland) would eventually prove successful and expand its holdings in North America.

## FOUNDING THE ENGLISH AMERICAN COLONIES

*Jamestown became the first permanent English settlement in what became the US. After the initial voyage of Columbus under the flag of Ferdinand and Isabella in 1492, Spanish maritime exploration expanded. In response, King Henry VII sponsored the voyage of John Cabot in 1497, providing the initial English claim for Newfoundland. However, as the Spanish established several colonies in the New World, England struggled. The infamous Roanoke colony, established 1585 by Sir Walter Raleigh in what is now North Carolina (then Virginia), survived only a few months before all inhabitants disappeared with no discernible trace left behind. The defeat of the Spanish Armada in 1588 seemed to swing the door wide open for English sailing, but still it would be 1607 before colonial permanency came with Jamestown. These colonists nearly starved until the leadership of Captain John Smith, reorganization, and the cultivation of tobacco as a cash crop brought sustainable economic success. Finally, other English colonists began to successfully follow in New England and the Chesapeake Bay area to join Virginia. With these colonies, the English established themselves in North America.*

The colonization of the future US proved to be slow at first but grew steadily throughout the 17th Century. The following is the chronological order of colonial establishments in what became the US:
- Jamestown became first permanent English settlement in North America (Virginia), 1607
- Plymouth (Massachusetts), 1620
- New Hampshire, 1623
- Lord Baltimore founded Maryland, 1624
- Puritans founded Connecticut, 1636

Insidious Changes

- Roger Williams founded Rhode Island, 1636
- Carolinas, 1653 (would be divided into North and South when the Crown took control in 1729)
- New Amsterdam fell to the English and was renamed New York, 1664
- New Sweden also transferred to the English and renamed Delaware, 1664
- New Jersey (divided from New York), 1664
- William Penn founded Pennsylvania, 1682
- James Oglethorpe founded Georgia, 1732

Only the coastal areas remained relatively free from attacks by challengers. As English/British sea power rose, their trade flourished, and their colonies grew. For many years, the French would challenge for supremacy on the waves, but this rarely hindered the American colonies. On land, the situation proved to be a bit different. The French had Indian allies to the west, so the continuing expansion of English/British colonies from the coast brought inevitable conflict. Specifically, the Ohio River Valley proved to be the area of conflict that would prove decisive in North America. However, this took several years and would do much to shape the mentality of the typical American colonial.

## THE ROAD TO BRITISH DOMINATION IN NORTH AMERICA

*After the discovery of the Americas, the race was on for European monarchs to grab territory and extract resources. The Spanish and Portuguese were first out of the gate, followed by the French. The English lagged behind; even the Swedes and the Dutch established settlements in North America as the English plodded along. As France and Spain took the lion's share of territory in North America, the English/British consolidated on the American East Coast, mostly surrounded by the French. During the 18th Century, the conflicts between the two colonial giants began to increase in intensity. In the final showdown ending in 1763, the British would stand as the undisputed authority on the North American continent with the French defeated and the Spanish in decline.*

Insidious Changes

The struggle for power in Europe began to spill over into North America, as well as other colonies. Rival European powers vied for dominance for many years as a result of the global expansion that began in the late 15th Century, exploding in the following century.

Italians had been active in trade to the Far East since the adventures of Marco Polo during the 13th Century. When Christopher Columbus sailed the ocean blue in 1492, he sought a shorter (and more efficient) route to the Far East, specifically India, to move the raw materials of luxury items, including silk and spices (used to extend the life of meats), to Europe. Efficiency would increase profits, of course, and the prospects must have seemed inviting to Ferdinand and Isabella of the newly united country we know as Spain. Although Columbus did not reach the Far East, he landed in a new (to Europeans) environment full of potential for the expanding civilization of Western Europe.

The Spanish, being the first, proved to be the most organized, and profited the most with early colonies. Adventurers such as Hernando Cortez sought gold for the crown and themselves. Columbus opened the door for the Spanish monarchy, then the Portuguese and French, to claim various geographical jurisdictions in the New World, as well as bringing Catholic Christianity to the inhabitants. In this mix, the English lagged in their efforts.

As mentioned previously, the English successfully established the Jamestown colony of Virginia in 1607. This successful settlement came after several non-productive voyages and unsuccessful attempts at colonization.[8] The religious impetus to leave England in the 1620s and 1630s resulted in a proliferation of colonies in New England. These colonies proved to be very independent: the New England town hall meeting is a vestige of this early independence and self-government and an enduring feature of the American political landscape. Eventually, the English established themselves not only in Virginia but also in the Mid-Atlantic area as well as New England and into the Carolinas. The island nation became a colonial player, and

---

[8] In 1587, the first English colonist, Virginia Dare, was born in America. Virginia Dare and all the colonists of Roanoke had disappeared three years later when John White, her grandfather, returned in an effort to replenish the colony. Roanoke Island is now in Dare County, North Carolina.

Insidious Changes

the English entered the fray for territory and wealth in the New World as the rivalries among European monarchies became continual.

The eruption of the Glorious Revolution brought a response from Stuart cousin Louis XIV of France. The War of the Grand Alliance (or League of Augsburg) in Europe ran concurrently with King William's War in North America (1689-97). In North America, New England could hardly wait to throw off the Stuart-appointed governor Sir Edmund Andros and reinstate their traditional institutions of elected, local control.[9] Against the French, the struggle resulted in a British-Iroquois alliance. Strategically, the British attempted to take Quebec, and the French had an objective to take Boston. Both plans failed, but the English did hold Port Royal in Nova Scotia for a time. However, in the end, the war proved to be mostly indecisive.

From 1702 until 1713, Queen Anne's War in North America and the War of Spanish Succession (British, Dutch, and Austrians vs. French and Spanish) in Europe brought British gains. The British again captured Port Royal in 1710, but under the Treaty of Utrecht, France retained New France, Cape Breton, and Prince Edward Island (all in Canada). The British gained Newfoundland, Hudson Bay, and Acadia (also in Canada).[10]

War again broke out in 1744-8 with King George's War: the War of Austrian Succession in Europe (1740-8; Austria, Prussia, France, and Spain vs. Britain and Austria). In North America, colonial forces from New England took the Louisbourg fortress in Nova Scotia (1745). However, Britain returned this victory with the Treaty of Aix-la-Chapelle, causing animosity among the colonists.

All of these struggles in North America culminated in the French and Indian War (1754-63), which in turn, grew into the expansive Seven Years' War in Europe (1756-63, Britain and Prussia vs. France, Spain, Austria, Russia, and Sweden). Benjamin Franklin drafted the Albany Plan of Union for the colonies to coordinate their efforts against the French (the plan would not be adopted by the colonists or British). The British and colonial forces, including George Washington, attempted to move the French out of the Ohio River

---

[9] Charles II began and James II completed an attempt to consolidate royal rule over the colonies of New England. This met with American resistance throughout the effort.

[10] During this struggle, the Act of Union in 1707 formed the United Kingdom of Great Britain and Ireland (therefore, we refer to Britain and the British).

Valley (the Iroquois would eventually help drive the French out of the region).  At first unsuccessful, the British finally captured Louisbourg in 1758, Quebec in 1759, Montreal in 1760, and proved victorious in the West Indies in 1762.  The fighting ended with the Treaty of Paris in 1763 (whereby the French abandoned French Canada).  The British ruled the continent, indeed were the global superpower ruling the seas and colonies across the globe.  Years later, in 1920, the British Empire would reach its peak of global expanse: the sun never set on the British Empire!

Insidious Changes

Insidious Changes

# III: FORMULATING A NEW GOVERNING PHILOSOPHY

## PUSHING THE AMERICANS TO INDEPENDENCE

*After an overwhelming victory by the British in North America, the London crowd in Parliament began to exert a new level of authority over the 13 colonies that would become the United States. The colonists of the time resisted various measures for a decade before the Second Continental Congress declared independence and a new nation on July 4, 1776.*

If we move our time travel up 140 years, we find ourselves as colonial militia soldiers fighting alongside the regular professional army known as Redcoats. We defend our homes with all our abilities, and we protect ourselves as English subjects against the rival French. Some of us would never return to our farms, but we know it is worth it. The English king holds our legal right to land and other private property, gives us avenues of trade, and provides all the governmental mechanisms we needed to prosper. Who knows what the French king would do, so we must take up arms and defend our Crown!

After years of struggle, we begin to receive very definitive news that British forces are now proving to be victorious. The French are retreating in the western lands and lost their stronghold of Quebec. Soon, we are again receiving definitive news that the French had abandoned direct engagement in North America, and would surrender not only their western lands to the Mississippi River but also Canada. The possibility for the future expansion of American colonies seems nearly boundless!

To the victor belong the spoils, so the saying goes, but so does the bill (wars have been, and continue to be, expensive propositions). After years of defending the colonies, Parliament sought to have the colonists pay a more substantial portion of the war bill. In 1764 Parliament passed the Sugar Act to raise government revenue, and in 1765 they passed the Stamp Act: the colonies responded with the Stamp Act Congress. The Americans protested so vehemently Parliament repealed the egregious act the next year. Parliament

~ 27 ~

regrouped in 1767 and passed the Townshend Acts threatening the Massachusetts legislature with disbandment along with other punitive measures.[11]  A short three years later (1770), Parliament repealed these acts after the Boston Massacre.  A British captain and eight soldiers were tried for this incident, but all were acquitted with the exception of two soldiers found guilty of murder (their convictions were reduced to manslaughter through a legal loophole), all were acquitted.  To put it mildly, the colonists were not pleased.

Throughout this period of strife between the colonies and Parliament, the seedbed of independence would be unknowingly cultivated.  Despite their dissatisfaction with Parliament and its actions, a majority of colonists prior to 1776 did not seriously mount any movement toward separation from the motherland, but the seedbed had begun to be cultivated.  In late 1767, John Dickinson began to pen thoughts of the colonists removing themselves from the corruption of British politics with his widely disseminated "Letters from a Pennsylvania Farmer," and such events as the Boston Massacre grew colonial discontent with the London-dominated status quo.  Even as Committees of Correspondence (to bring unity of purpose beginning in 1772) branched into Committees of Inspection (or Observation, the enforcement arm of the Continental Association designed to boycott imports), and Committees of Safety (to safeguard militia stockpiles), the idea of independence grew slowly.  During these years, dissatisfaction grew in the colonies, and Parliament did not seriously address the sources of discontent.

---

[11] Named after the Chancellor of the Exchequer, Charles Townshend who suggested the measures.  The New York Restraining Act required the quartering of troops which the colonists insisted amounted to taxation without representation.  The Revenue Act authorized "writs of assistance" or general warrants.  The Indemnity Act reduced taxes for the British East India Company when importing to Britain, which could be turned around, an attempt to reduce the price and overcome the black market in the tea trade (a Dutch money-maker).  The Commissioners of Customs Act moved the Customs Board for North America from London to Boston.  The Vice Admiralty Court Act (not always included) came a year later than the others and after the sudden death of Townshend: it took customs violations from colonial courts to Royal naval courts where judges could receive five percent of fines and were not subject to trial by jury.  Technically, this was a regulation as its approval came through the Lords Commissioners of His Majesty's Treasury (and royal approval) rather than with a vote of Parliament.

Insidious Changes

Events became even more heated beginning in 1773 when Parliament passed the Tea Act to save the British East India Company from bankruptcy. The Massachusetts colonists responded with the Boston Tea Party, tossing the taxed commodity into the Boston Harbor. In 1774, Parliament passed what they called the Coercive Acts, which the colonists labeled the Intolerable Acts, all designed to be a direct punishment of Massachusetts. The acts consisted of the:

- Boston Port Act intended to close the Port of Boston until the lost revenue from the Boston Tea Party could be recovered;
- Massachusetts Government Act which restricted self-government in the colony;
- Impartial Administration of Justice Act which allowed the royal governor to change the venue for British officials or soldiers to England which would incur a great cost to any Americans wishing to testify against them; and
- Quartering Act which allowed the royal governor to house British soldiers within colonial accommodations by decree.

Other colonists outside Massachusetts cast a wary eye on these political restrictions in New England. Add to this the Quebec Act, which also seemed to threaten political restrictions as well as the westward expansion for the American colonies, and the revolutionary fever began to grow to a higher level. In response, the colonial leaders called the First Continental Congress during September of 1774. During this meeting, tensions continued to rise, and some essential precedents were set.

In this first congress leading to revolution, the delegates decided to have one vote per colony rather than dividing their votes proportionately by population. This idea of the separate units retaining autonomy while acting together would endure as the colonies found their unifying identity.[12] However, before this issue

---

[12] The idea of states having their sovereignty and acting together in unity is reflected in the 1783 Treaty of Paris, Article I which read, "His Britannic Majesty acknowledges the said United States, viz., New Hampshire, Massachusetts Bay, Rhode Island and Providence Plantations, Connecticut, New York, New Jersey, Pennsylvania, Maryland, Virginia, North Carolina, South Carolina and Georgia, to be free sovereign and independent states, that he treats with them as such, and for himself, his heirs, and successors, relinquishes all claims to the government, propriety, and territorial rights of the same and every part thereof." Retrieved from, https://avalon.law.yale.edu/18th_century/paris.asp.

Insidious Changes

could be addressed, the Continental Congress had a growing problem on their hands.

On April 19, 1775, the situation took a dramatic turn as colonists squared off against British regulars at Lexington and Concord (Massachusetts). The American militiamen fired, "The shot heard 'round the world." Quickly, the Second Continental Congress convened while fighting continued. At Bunker Hill[13] (mostly fought on Breed's Hill), the Patriots inflicted heavy casualties on the British as Congress passed legislation to establish the Continental Army with George Washington in command. Even at this point, Congress sent the Olive Branch Petition to King George III, but he refused to look at the document and declared the Americans in open rebellion. A long war had begun.

In January 1776, the publication of *Common Sense* by Thomas Paine increased the clamor for colonial independence. Paine made a convincing argument that the time for American independence from the Crown had arrived.[14] Coupled with Locke's *Treatises*, the British denial of rights in America seemed unjustifiable. As the historian Bernard Bailyn outlined, these ideas of liberty circulated throughout the colonies with pamphleteering.[15] During 1776, events moved in rapid succession, and the colonies ultimately declared their independence. Declaring independence is one thing, but the trick would be securing that independence against the most powerful fighting force on the planet.

---

[13] The Battle of Bunker Hill inflicted heavy losses on the British, and the Americans withdrew only after running out of ammunition. The British "victory" inspired the Patriot cause in all colonies, and made the British re-evaluate their strategy. Eventually in the following March, the British would remove themselves from Boston; however, much to Washington's chagrin, the British would occupy New York City throughout the entire conflict.

[14] The contribution of Paine to American independence can hardly be overstated. Besides *Common Sense*, he penned *American Crisis* in the Continental Army's darkest moments reminding them that, "Tyranny like hell is not easily conquered; yet . . . the harder the conflict the more glorious the victory." He went back to England and wrote The *Rights of Man* which resulted in his banishment to France. In France he became a prisoner during the Reign of Terror. While in a cell, Paine wrote *The Age of Reason*, an attack on organized religion that left him with few friends in America and certainly helped to diminish his legacy in most histories.

[15] Bernard Bailyn, *The Ideological Origins of the American Revolution*, expanded edition, Belknap Press, Cambridge, MA, 1992.

# AMERICAN CHALLENGES AND FINAL VICTORY

*More than anything else attributable to human action, tenacity won the Revolutionary War. After the initial encouraging efforts in Massachusetts, the Patriots would have a much tougher road ahead of them. Washington crossed the Delaware River to surprise the British forces after a very challenging year in 1776. The subsequent victories would bolster the spirits of the Patriots, but the Continental Army proved to be difficult to hold together during the winter months. However, with the return of spring, the ranks were filled again, and Washington continued his campaign. Years of struggle and stalemate tested the resolve of the Americans, but the entry of France as an ally helped the Continental Army remain a viable fighting force. Finally, when opportunity knocked in the fall of 1781, Washington penned the British down at Yorktown. The British would abandon the fight at that point, and the US officially gained recognition in 1783.*

Once the fighting started between the Patriots and the Red Coats, the initial battles occurred quickly. The events of 1776 included:

- The British evacuation of Boston after an American victory in March. The British targeted New York and Washington would move the Continental Army south to face the Redcoats.
- In July, Congress adopted the "Declaration of Independence." The Committee of Five, mostly Thomas Jefferson, penned the justification for American independence.
- After a defeat on Long Island and White Plains, New York, Washington began his tactic of avoiding face-to-face confrontation with the British. The Redcoats would occupy New York for the remainder of the fighting.
- Congress abandoned the capital in Philadelphia for Baltimore.
- Finally, on Christmas Eve, Washington crossed the Delaware River and surprised the Hessians (German mercenaries fighting for the British) at Trenton, New Jersey. A follow up American victory came a few days later at Princeton.

The victory at Trenton proved to be a crucial victory for the morale of the Continental Army, and the war for independence became the

Insidious Changes

destiny of the Americans.  In January 1777, Washington achieved another New Jersey victory at Princeton, but the harsh winter took its toll.  The Continental Army shrank in the unforgiving conditions; however, troops returned in the spring.  The young Marquis de Lafayette arrived to offer his free services to Washington (he became an extremely trusted advisor).  After a back-and-forth campaign, and a major loss at Brandywine Creek, the Americans scored a huge victory at Saratoga, New York, which led to French recognition and aid in the struggle against Britain.

During another harsh winter at Valley Forge in 1778, the Prussian Baron von Steuben arrived to drill the Americans into a cohesive, professional unit.  Congress rejected a peace offer that held all demands except independence.  As the official American ambassador, Benjamin Franklin traveled to France, successfully keeping them on the American side throughout the remainder of the conflict.  Although things looked up, the British began a successful southern campaign that plagued the Americans.

At Charleston in 1780, the Americans suffered their worst defeat, but a Continental Army rebellion would be subdued.  Subsequently, Nathaniel Greene led British commander Lord Cornwallis on a devastating goose chase throughout the South.  Finally, the American victory at Cowpens, South Carolina (1781) set off a series of events that ended the war.

After the American success at Cowpens, Cornwallis decided to concentrate on Virginia.  The French fleet led by Count de Grasse moved toward the Chesapeake Bay.  The movement of the French fleet led to Washington and French General Rochambeau undertaking a campaign to trap the British general at Yorktown, Virginia.[16]  In October, the British surrendered: the fighting ended, but peace proved more elusive.

In early 1781, Congress began to operate under the Articles of Confederation (adopted in 1777 and finally ratified in March 1781). The Confederation Congress would negotiate with the British. Parliament voted to suspend military pursuits in America with a formal vote in February 1782.  Finally, in September 1783, and with the Continental Army having threatened mutiny in March (which

---

[16] American traitor Benedict Arnold warned General Cornwallis that British troops could be trapped on the peninsula around Yorktown but his advice fell on deaf ears.

Insidious Changes

Washington stopped with his commanding presence), the British and Americans agreed to the Treaty of Paris. Washington then voluntarily resigned his commission effective at the end of the year. Victory, peace, and a new country finally took its place on the world stage.


## THE FIRST AMERICAN CONSTITUTION

*The Second Continental Congress conducted the Revolutionary War and also wrote a constitution known as the Articles of Confederation. The Articles became the first constitution of the US from 1781-89.*

Since the Mayflower Compact of 1620, Americans have written down their rules of governing. At the time of the Declaration of Independence, the idea of written rules (written constitutions) had become well ingrained. So, with a prompt from the Continental Congress, independence from the king led to a flurry of state constitutions. Although these documents carried variations, some common themes also emerged, such as an emphasis of the individual over the state, a bill of rights, elected representatives, three distinct branches of government with a dominant legislature, and constitutional law being superior to statutory law.

Most states remained with the system they knew, which included a two-house, bicameral legislature. However, Pennsylvania went with a unicameral legislature, one house, an annual election schedule, legislation that would be proposed and then sit several months for public debate before the final vote, and very weak and dispersed executive power. In all the new states, their blueprints set the legislature as the dominant force, and the constitution would underlie all governmental action. However, our first national constitution, the Articles of Confederation, tended to favor the Pennsylvania model of a weak executive and a unicameral legislature.

The Continental Congress authorized the drafting of a new constitution that Congress completed in November 1777. It contained an outline that established (or more rightly said, retained) Congress as the supreme entity in the new confederation. The Congress consisted of a unicameral (one house) body with equal representation of each state (that's right, state representation). It gave Congress the power to declare war and make peace. It could negotiate treaties.

~ 33 ~

However, the Confederation Congress lacked several powers considered essential to a strong government. The deficiencies included:

- No direct authority to collect taxes.
- Lack of financial control as states could still coin their own money.
- No ability to regulate commerce.
- Ineffective executive authority.

Although from the very beginnings of the US with the First Continental Congress, states had acted as autonomous units with a unified goal, the end of the war brought problems resulting from divisions of interest. These problems ultimately led to the demise of the Articles. However, they reflected much of the Founders' thoughts and influences. Limited and small government could be controlled. The dangers of too much central authority had been expressed at this time by the Scotsman Adam Smith, who illustrated how government-controlled and crippled economic activity rather than letting it flourish naturally. The Frenchman Voltaire also challenged the status quo concerning a lack of religious freedom and judicial justice in his homeland. The Founders shared these sentiments, so they kept central authority to a minimum. However, despite the hindrance of inadequate authority to implement effective policy, the Confederation Congress did chalk up some positives.

Congress forbade slavery in the Northwest Territories. This expression against involuntary servitude did have the provision that a slave would be returned to the slave owner. The provision avoided a safe-haven for escaped slaves while making a statement about the spread of slavery in new territories, at least for that period in time. However, containing slavery as an institution would remain as a source of tension for the US as it grew across the continent.

Also, the Land Ordinance of 1785 provided for the survey (Public Land Survey System) and sale of federal land. The Northwest Ordinance of 1787 also ensured that the new states north of the Ohio River would be equal in status to the original thirteen, and also solidified the process for statehood:

1. At first, a territory functioned with an appointed governor, secretary, and three judges.
2. The territory then elected a legislature.

~ 34 ~

3. Finally, the territory submitted a constitution to Congress for approval.

Despite these positives, problems persisted and compounded. Trade with Britain was disrupted: surpluses grew, and prices fell. The Confederation Congress defaulted on Continental debt, and Revolutionary War veterans became irritated. Daniel Shays, along with his Massachusetts followers, wanted tax relief, a moratorium on debt collection, and an end of imprisonment for debt. In January 1787, Shays' followers moved on Springfield and Boston. The Massachusetts militia defeated the rebels, but the armed action sent a fright through many political leaders. Finally, Congress called an emergency meeting for May.

## RESPONDING TO THE FAILING ARTICLES

*The Philadelphia Convention during the summer of 1787 became the Constitutional Convention as the delegates decided that a major overhaul of the US government was in order. They spent the summer ironing out details and their differences, finally breaking in September with a new proposal for the consideration of the states.*

The Founders faced a critical crisis with the failure of the Articles of Confederation. In 1786, the Annapolis Convention, called to discuss deficiencies of the Articles of Confederation, fell short of full attendance from the states. The delegates from five states recommended that Congress call another meeting in 1787 to amend the Articles, and this time delegates from nearly all states (Rhode Island proved to be the exception) attended after some external stimulus known as Shays' Rebellion.

Revolutionary War veterans had become irritated with economic upheaval. Most uprisings withered rather quickly, but Daniel Shays and followers in Massachusetts persisted. They wanted tax relief, a moratorium on debt collection, and an end to imprisonment for debt. Beginning in August 1786, the rebellion became serious in January 1787 when Shays' followers moved on Springfield and Boston. As noted above, the Massachusetts militia defeated the rebels, but they sent many political leaders took the waning: George Washington even returned to public life as a delegate for Virginia.

~ 35 ~

Immediately, the delegates went to work choosing Washington as the convention's president and proposing two plans:

Virginia Plan: introduced by Edmund Randolph and James Madison, this plan provided for a bicameral legislature (both houses based on population), and separate executive, legislative, and judicial branches.

New Jersey Plan: William Paterson introduced a revision of the Articles. It provided for equal representation of the states in a unicameral legislature while expanding the powers of Congress to regulate commerce, levy certain taxes, and name an executive and a supreme court.

The delegates argued for many weeks. Finally, the Connecticut (or Great) Compromise brought a resolution. It proposed a bicameral legislature (one house of equal representation, the other by population), three branches, and expanded Congressional powers to include authority to levy taxes, coin money, regulate commerce, and maintain the national defense.

Additional compromises followed: The Three-fifths Compromise for purposes of representation (slaves would be counted as 3/5s a person for determining the number of representatives a state had in Congress). Also, the question of the president being elected by the people or chosen by Congress found resolution within the Electoral College, where states chose electors to elect an executive. Initially, the candidate with the most electoral votes won the presidency, and the runner-up won the vice-presidency (this would be changed with the 12$^{th}$ Amendment, today the two run as a team).

All this debate ended in a federal government composed of three branches: each possessing powers with checks and balances over the other branches. Every government class worth its salt covers these principles of separation of powers and checks and balances:

- Congress passes laws;
- the president signs or vetoes those laws;
- Congress can override the veto;
- the Senate approves presidential appointments; and
- the Supreme Court determines the constitutionality of laws passed by Congress.

This innovative system has proven enduring and has been instrumental in preserving limited government in the US.

Insidious Changes

# BASIC FEATURES OF THE CONSTITUTION

*With the Constitution, the Founders placed governmental authority as the "consent of the governed" rather than a full-blown democracy. Many of the convention delegates were students of antiquity and very familiar with the problems of direct democracy as described by Aristotle. In their quest for "a more perfect union," they blended the consent of the governed with limited direct participation to overcome the indiscretions of direct democracy that could turn into mob rule and violations of fundamental rights through a tyranny of the majority.*

The Constitution provides for limited government incorporated through the separation of powers and a system of checks and balances. Congress, the president, and the judicial branch all have specific functions and powers that maintain the balance of power and force compromise, thereby limiting the scope of government. Just imagine the strength of the president if he had no check from Congress. Likewise, what if Congress had no review of constitutionality from the Supreme Court? Also, often overlooked is the fact that the states are also a part of this system.

The states are guaranteed powers in Article V, which allow them to call a convention to propose amendments, and a supermajority of states must approve amendments. Originally, state legislatures appointed senators providing federal representation for the various states. The original Constitution gave a few specified, enumerated powers to the federal government, and most powers remained with the states. Many of these state powers have eroded over time, but the notion of three branches and spreading power between them has persisted. A list of federal powers and other stipulations are contained in the Constitution's seven articles which are summarized below (this is not a complete catalog; the list includes the most important features):

ARTICLE I: THE LEGISLATURE - qualifications, powers, and limitations

~ 37 ~

- Representatives to be 25 years old, seven years a citizen and live within the state they represent; two-year term
- Senators to be 30 years old, nine years a citizen, and live within the state they serve; six-year term
- Revenue bills must begin in the House of Representatives
- Section 8 (enumerated or delegated powers)
  - Lay and collect taxes
  - Borrow money
  - Regulate international and interstate trade, and trade with the Indian tribes
  - Establish rules for naturalization and bankruptcy
  - Coin money, regulate its value
  - Establish patents and copyrights
  - Establish courts inferior to the Supreme Court (Judiciary Act of 1795)
  - Establish maritime law
  - Declare war
  - Maintain the army (may not appropriate for more than two years at a time)
  - Maintain the navy
  - Regulate military forces
  - Call up and maintain the militia to enforce laws, preserve peace, and repel invasion
  - To legislate for the District of Columbia, and operate and maintain other federal property
  - "To make all laws which are necessary and proper for carrying into Execution the foregoing Powers and all other Powers vested by this Constitution in the Government of the United States, or any Department or Officer thereof ."
- Prohibited Powers of Congress (Section 9)
  - No suspension of Habeas Corpus unless in time of rebellion or invasion
  - No bills of attainder (punishment by Congress) or ex post facto laws (after the fact)
  - No direct taxes (changed by 16th Amendment)
  - No taxes on state exports

- o No preference to ports of one state over another, no taxes on ships from other states
  - o No money spent unless appropriated and publicly disclosed
  - o No titles of nobility
- Prohibited powers to the states (Section 10)
  - o No foreign treaties
  - o No declarations of war
  - o No coinage of money
  - o No ex post facto laws (after the fact)
  - o No titles of nobility
  - o No taxes on interstate commerce other than inspection
  - o Cannot maintain a standing army or navy

ARTICLE II: THE EXECUTIVE – Establishes qualifications, powers, and duties

- President must be a natural-born citizen, at least 35 years old, residing in the US at least 14 years, four-year term
- Establishment of the Electoral College[17]
- President acts as chief executive and commander-in-chief of the armed forces
- President will enforce the laws of the US
- May grant pardons
- President may make treaties (with the consent of the Senate)
- President may make appointments (with advice and consent of the Senate)

---

[17] There is debate today concerning the relevancy of the Electoral College. Some critics use the argument that the Founders did not trust the selection of this important officeholder to the voters. Of course, the institution has changed over time, and today voters select the president through the college. The two strongest arguments for the Electoral College are structural and the weighting of votes. First, we only have state voting systems, there is no national mechanism for elections and the Electoral College reports the state vote to Congress. Secondly, but probably most importantly, is that the Electoral College allows some leveling between high population states vs. low population states. Alaskans have a reason to vote and support the system because their vote is weighted against heavily populated states like California. A pure popular vote would boil the selection of the president to about ten states, with the rest of the country just receiving exercise and little representation.

Insidious Changes

- Text of the presidential oath
- Vice President will serve as President of the Senate

ARTICLE III: JUDICIARY
- Established the Supreme Court,
- Congress allowed to construct inferior courts (Judiciary Act of 1795 enacted under this provision)
- Right to trial by jury guaranteed
- Appointment for life without reduction in pay

ARTICLE IV: FULL FAITH AND CREDIT – Citizens of one state have all rights and privileges in other states

ARTICLE V: AMENDMENT PROCESS - Describes the methods of amending the Constitution
Amendments may be:
1. proposed by 2/3s of both Houses, or
2. national convention requested by 2/3s of state legislatures, and
3. amendments must be ratified by 3/4s of state legislatures, or
4. 3/4s of state conventions (conventions have been used only once with the repeal of Prohibition).

ARTICLE VI: SUPREMACY CLAUSE - Laws in conflict with state statutes and treaties of the US are superior to those of the states.

ARTICLE VII: RATIFICATION - Nine states required to ratify the Constitution and for it to become functional. (For dates of ratification, see below.)

Finally, the institution of slavery garnered little mention in the Constitution as the Southern states would not have signed on if the Northerners had banned slavery. Of course, slavery had been banned in new states formed in the Northwest Territory by the Confederation Congress. The Constitution contained a provision for restriction of the slave trade in subsequent years. Congress

~ 40 ~

took advantage of this provision in 1807 when it designated 1808 as the year to end slave trading in the District of Columbia. However, at this point, the South had a self-sustaining slave population caught in perpetual servitude from generation to generation. In the end, the conflict would be left for another day, and as we know, that day of resolution proved to be the bloody Civil War.

## ADOPTING THE CONSTITUTION

*The proposal of a new constitution moved quickly through the states for ratification, and the new government came into being in 1789. However, the process hosted a serious debate about the assurances that the federal government would remain limited in practice. This debate had an impact on the First Congress, which quickly passed and offered the Bill of Rights for ratification.*

Article VII of the Constitution called for state conventions to adopt the proposed form of government. It also specified that the affirmation of nine states would signify the adoption of the Constitution.

George Mason and Edmund Randolph left Philadelphia without signing the proposed constitution. Randolph cited a lack of a bill of rights and protection for the individual. Patrick Henry had concerns about the phrase "We the people," and continued to favor "We the states," as originally penned, but changed in the final draft by Gouverneur Morris.[18]

The opposition coalesced into the Anti-Federalists while the proponents became the Federalists. Being suspicious of increased centralized authority, the Anti-Federalists quickly penned their concerns. Criticisms such as "Letters from the Federal Farmer" warned that a small and powerful elite would control a central mechanism and threaten the freedom so recently won from British rule.[19] The president would become the new monarch, the judiciary

---

[18] With the Article VII stipulation of nine states constituting the adoption of the Constitution, the usual list of all states would run counter to this provision.
[19] Both opponents and proponents of the Constitution tried to grab the title

Insidious Changes

too independent, and states would be crushed. Writing as *Brutus*, George Mason, and Richard Henry Lee warned that liberty could easily slip away under this new configuration of power. The debate also caused constitutional supporters to pen their thoughts.

The *Federalist Papers* published under the name *Publius* (Alexander Hamilton, James Madison, and John Jay), laid out the positive argument for the Constitution. As a guiding light into the Founders' thoughts and intentions, these writings are still considered by many to be the most significant American political writings ever published. These 85 editorials would later be compiled into a book and became the "Bible" to defend the new constitution. In many American Government textbooks and courses, two are almost always emphasized. *Federalist No. 10* and *Federalist No. 51*, both by Madison, are included here as quick summaries. However, there is no substitute for reading the full essays.

Madison wrote *Federalist No. 10* to argue the advantages of a large republic. Madison asserted factions ruined the Articles of Confederation, but the new constitutional arrangement would solve this problem. The unity of a large geographic area, Madison argued, allowed people to make decisions, to agree and disagree, but yet no one "faction" could take full control of government. People could have their debates and disagreements, but no one faction could grab total control of all the ruling mechanisms. Unlike the Frenchman Montesquieu, Madison believed that a large republic should be preferable to a small republic because a large republic with several states would thwart efforts of a small group to gain power.

*Federalist No. 51,* Madison provided his rationale for developing the system of checks and balances as well as the separation of powers to retain self-government. Here he penned his famous lines asserting that if men were angels, we would have no need for government. Similarly, if angels ruled men, we would not need government, but neither is the situation of the world. We must allow governance because men are not angels, and we need to have checks on a government consisting of flawed humanity.

Arguing that ambition can frustrate ambition, Madison asserted that the multiple divisions of power in the US act to preserve the

---

Federalist, but the constitutional proponents won the day. Labeling was important even in the 18th Century!

Insidious Changes

liberty of the people. In the large republic of the US, the people are protected first and foremost by having power divided between two governments: the federal and their states. Then the multiple branches of the legislature (which is divided), executive, and judiciary at the two levels divide power and again frustrate would-be ruling factions. The legislative branch is the most powerful, and as a result, should be divided itself with separate procedures to ensure that abuse is frustrated. The two governmental entities, as well as the separation of powers within the branches, will preserve liberty.

The Federalists had the early momentum, and ratification came rather quickly until Massachusetts. There the Anti-Federalist opposition gained enough ground that the ratifying convention approved the governmental changes, but also requested a bill of rights. Virginia and New York soon followed suit with a call similar to that of Massachusetts. These outcries proved to be the primary contribution of the Anti-Federalists, and the first ten amendments, proposed by the First Congress, provided the protection of personal liberty Mason sought.

### Constitution Ratification Chronology

> 1787: Delaware 12/1; Pennsylvania 12/12; New Jersey 12/18
> 1788: Georgia 1/2; Connecticut 1/9; Massachusetts 2/6; Maryland 4/28; S. Carolina 5/23; New Hampshire 6/21[20]; Virginia 6/25; New York 7/26
> 1789: N. Carolina 7/11 and 7/21
> 1790: Rhode Island 5/29
> 1791: 1/10 Vermont ratifies Constitution and applies for admission to the Union[21]

## THE BILL OF RIGHTS: COMPLETING THE

---

[20] On June 21, 1788, New Hampshire became the ninth state to ratify the Constitution, but the reality of the nation without Virginia and New York seemed bleak to put it mildly. However, both soon followed in ratification.
[21] Vermont would be accepted into the union in 1791. The Vermont Republic had been proclaimed in 1777, the first autonomous republic to be admitted to the US: the others are California, Texas, and Hawaii.

~ 43 ~

# 1787 CONSTITUTION

*As mentioned previously, the First Congress sent 12 articles to the states in 1789 for consideration to bolster the guarantee of individual liberties and further define the limited scope of the federal government. The states ratified ten of the articles by the end of 1791.*

As the First Congress convened, Madison proposed nine amendments to the Constitution in answer to the Anti-Federalist call for a bill of rights. Madison heard the protests during ratification and believed they had to be addressed. After all, inherited rights were part of the impetus to war, and had developed into part of the American governing tradition. As early as 1641, the Body of Liberties in Massachusetts reflected the idea of individual rights and included such provisions as the right to due process, trial by jury, the prohibition of double jeopardy, and prohibition of cruel and unusual punishment. Madison's original proposal would be somewhat altered in committee, but then quickly moved through Congress. The body settled on 12 proposals sent these to the states on September 25, 1789. These articles were:

1. The number of representatives for the House would be divided proportionately and limited in number.
2. Any raise passed by Congress for itself will not be implemented until the next Congress.
3. Freedom of speech, religion, and press; right to assembly and petition guaranteed.
4. Right to bear arms.
5. No forced quartering of troops in time of peace.
6. Security against unreasonable search and seizure, probable cause must be demonstrated for warrant to be issued (no general warrants).
7. Criminal trial rights explained, right to avoid testifying against self, due process.
8. Right to speedy trial in criminal cases, trial by jury, face accuser.
9. Right to trial by jury in civil case and appeal of decision.
10. Freedom from excessive bails, fines, and punishment.
11. If not listed does not deny rights to people.
12. Those rights not listed reserved to states or people.

~ 44 ~

Articles 3-12 became the first ten amendments, the Bill of Rights. After receiving the 12 articles in 1789, the states wasted little time. In slightly over two years, December 15, 1791, (rocket speed in political terms), the Bill of Rights had been ratified by 3/4s of the states (see ratification list below). The finalized Bill of Rights guaranteeing certain rights that we know today is as follows:

1st Amendment-freedom of speech, religion, and press; right to assembly and petition guaranteed

2nd Amendment-right to bear arms

3rd Amendment-no forced quartering of troops in time of peace

4th Amendment-security against unreasonable search and seizure, probable cause must be demonstrated for a warrant to be issued (no general warrants)

5th Amendment-criminal trial rights explained, right to avoid testifying against self, due process

6th Amendment-right to a speedy trial in criminal cases, trial by jury, face accuser

7th Amendment-right to trial by jury in civil case and appeal of a decision

8th Amendment-freedom from excessive bails, fines, and punishment

9th Amendment-if not listed does not deny rights to people

10th Amendment-those rights not listed reserved to states or people.

The first proposed article has not been adopted as an amendment but has been implemented in various bills that have passed Congress (the House of Representatives is currently holding at 435 divided proportionately on each census every ten years). In an interesting quirk, the 2nd Article became the 27th Amendment.[22] University of Texas sophomore Gregory Watson wrote a paper in 1982 arguing that without a date of expiration (sunset) on the proposal, the article could still be ratified by the states: he received a "C" grade for his efforts. Not to be denied, Watson began a campaign for adoption, which

---

[22] The order of ratification for the Bill of Rights was: New Jersey 11/20/1789; Maryland 12/19/1789; North Carolina 12/22/1789; South Carolina 1/19/1790; New Hampshire 1/25/1790; Delaware 1/28/1790; New York 2/24/1790; Pennsylvania 3/10/1790; Rhode Island 6/7/1790 (Arts. 1, 3-12); Vermont 11/3/1791; Virginia 12/15/1791.

successfully ended in 1992 with Missouri, Alabama, and Michigan all ratifying within three days in May.

The Bill of Rights solidified the individual as primary over the federal government. A far away (physically and philosophically) government would not take away the hard-earned victory for liberty from individuals and deny them their right to pursue happiness and well-being. The European philosopher Jean Jacques Rousseau had written about the chains of constraint on human activity, but now Americans, at least some Americans, had broken their chains.[23]

---

[23] There have been 17 more amendments adopted after the Bill of Rights. These were (with ratification date):

11th    Federal suits cannot be brought from citizens of one state against another state or from foreign citizens    (1795).
12th    President and Vice-President run on the same ticket (1804).
13th    Slavery prohibited (1865).
14th    Anyone born in the US is a citizen; due process and equal protection applies to the states (1868).
15th    Right to vote for all male citizens (1870).
16th    Authorized income tax (1913).
17th    Direct election of senators (1913).
18th    Prohibition (1919).
19th    Gave women the right to vote (1920).
20th    Presidential inaugurated on January 20; Congress convenes on January 3(1933).
21st    Prohibition repealed (1933).
22nd    A president is limited to two terms, or 10 years total if fulfilling another's term (1951).
23rd    Gave Washington, D.C. three electoral votes (1961).
24th    Poll taxes prohibited (1964).
25th    Clarified what constitutes presidential disability and how that can be determined by the cabinet, and also clarified succession to the presidency in case of vacancy (1967).
26th    Voting age moved from 21 to 18 (1971).
27th    A sitting Congress cannot vote itself a raise; an increase will apply to next the Congress (1992).

~ 46 ~

# IV: EARLY PRACTICES AND INTERPRETATIONS

## METHODS FOR CHANGING THE CONSTITUTION

*There are two ways to change the Constitution, formally and informally. The formal process requires amendments, a process which is quite cumbersome and difficult. The informal process consists of practice and interpretation, both of which become precedent and part of application for future governmental operations.*

Continuing our time travel journey, as Americans, we support George Washington to be our first president. He led us to victory over the abuses of the king and his appointees and proved that he would not follow a similar course when he had power. Also, he has proven himself to be a reformer, but not a radical. He is a landowner, he is in business, he is one of our kindred souls, and we can trust him! We need change and stability, and Washington has the steady hand to deliver both.

The chaos of the Articles period brought considerable uncertainty to the new nation. However, the Founders successfully navigated the hazards of a new nation and implemented a new outline for governing. As the first elections were held under the new constitutional format, the initial officeholders would change from philosophical constructionists to making their mark as practitioners.

The election of George Washington as the first president provided the final step to forming a practical unity for the new American nation. Washington would take his charge seriously and provided the platform for American survival, and even expansion. He carefully set precedents for the executive office of president, and carefully made sure that he did not overstep congressional authority. However, he would find limits to cooperation with the legislature, and as a result, would draw lines between the two branches. Mostly, subsequent presidents respected the boundaries set by Washington, but there were exceptions.

Jefferson would move quickly to purchase the Louisiana Territory from Napoleon before an unforeseen event of any kind could happen.

Insidious Changes

Abraham Lincoln would push the limits of executive authority during the very trying time of the Civil War. However, the 20th Century would bring a significant change.

First, Theodore Roosevelt threw off many constraints that had kept the federal government small and began to expand agencies, regulations, as well as size. Woodrow Wilson sat in the Oval Office as the Federal Reserve, national income tax, and direct election of senators became law. The Great Depression threw much of the previous caution out the window as Franklin Roosevelt implemented a permanently enlarged federal government through the New Deal and World War II. Lyndon Johnson would grow Washington, DC, even larger with the Great Society. As is historically evident, the presidency has served as a conduit for a larger federal government, but the executive has had help from the judiciary.

When John Marshall set the precedent of judicial review in 1803, the Supreme Court potentially became lawmakers in their own right. It took years for this aspect of power to fully develop, but judicial reinterpretation (activism) became the norm after FDR, only recently being trimmed in a conscious effort by presidents.[24] These informal changes have led to increasing rights for the criminally accused, legalization of abortion across the nation, as well as gay marriage. Today, the debate of who the president will appoint to the Court, and who will control the informal changes, is always a discussion during a presidential election.

## WASHINGTON'S PRECEDENTS

*The short-lived governing association of those favoring the new constitutional arrangements, the Federalists, did leave a significant mark on the US government. This significance is especially true of Washington as he set a precedent in all that he did: establishing a cabinet, exercising executive privilege, outlining a foreign policy, and much more.*

---

[24] With the Court's numerous rulings against the New Deal, FDR threatened to "pack" the Court with younger, i.e., more favorable, justices.

Insidious Changes

As noted above, with the Constitution ratified, the infant nation moved to federal elections. During the times of war and forming a new constitution, the new nation's leadership had turned to George Washington, and they remained with him to build a new government. A unanimous Electoral College vote chose Washington as the first president of the US.

Unfortunately, in today's world, an air of inevitability seems to surround this decision and the formation of a workable national union. As previously noted, during the ratification process, supporters and opponents of the Constitution quickly lined up on opposite sides. The Founders were quite aware that political factions could ruin a government: Madison cited this as the significant problem of the Articles. They also viewed Washington as the leader who would overcome this propensity to divide, no mean task.

Washington held some definite advantages. First, the leaders of the time all had a vested interest in success. They had been at the forefront of establishing a new nation, and they certainly wanted it to succeed. Secondly, as testified to by the vote, Washington held the respect and goodwill of the national political leadership. Although not the most prolific or articulate of the Founders (this would be a high bar indeed), he possessed the skills to "rally the troops" and point them in the right direction. Thirdly, his benevolence: by stepping down from the command of the Continental Army with the peace treaty that ended the war for independence, proved that he could be trusted with an enormous amount of power while resisting the temptation to abuse authority. Finally, he had the levelheaded common sense to establish precedents that would work for him and subsequent presidents.

For Washington, and all the Founders, a path between societal order and cohesiveness on the one hand, and individual liberty on the other proved to be a tricky task. Obviously, the first notion contained in the Articles to leave almost all power with the individual states in a confederation did not work well as the various states sought their particular good above all other goals. The unitary model of concentrating all power within the cabinet of Parliament, on the lines of Hamilton's proposal, went nowhere fast after the colonial experience of London's unchecked power. Therefore, a new, untested model of a federation, mostly a confederation at this point, would be launched with some powers delegated to the US government. The

Insidious Changes

danger the Founders identified would be the presidency, an office that held the potential of gathering executive and legislative power to itself, much like they had suffered under colonial rule. As a result, any legislative power of the executive is extremely limited under the Constitution, and other powers are checked. Washington proved through his actions that the system to provide national structure while allowing states retention of the historic authority they fought for during the struggle for independence could survive. However, the history of subsequent presidents would prove the Founders' suspicions to be correct. However, the system would be able to withstand a great deal of stress not only because of its structure, but also because of the boundaries set by George Washington, boundaries that would not be fully tested until the dawn of the 20th Century, and then only a bit at a time. Washington established the working limited government debated in Philadelphia, proving to be the "first in war, first in peace, and first in the hearts of his countrymen."[25]

## WASHINGTON, HAMILTON, AND THE INFANT US GOVERNMENT

*One of the least known and credited Founders, Alexander Hamilton, served as a delegate in Philadelphia and the first Secretary of the Treasury under Washington. He put the US financial house in order, helped solidify the legitimate financing of the US Government, and set economic policy for a future of economic growth based on the growing industrial revolution.*

As noted in the preceding section, everything Washington did set a precedent. As the first president, he set the tone for an office that many feared might overwhelm all rivals for power. Washington formed a modest group of advisors and administrators, the cabinet, to help him conduct the daily business of governing. Thomas Jefferson, the first Secretary of State, rounded out by Henry Knox, Secretary of War, and Edmund Jennings Randolph, the Attorney General (although not an official cabinet department until 1870). Alexander

---

[25] Fellow Virginian, politician, and soldier Henry "Light-Horse Harry" Lee wrote this eulogy to Washington upon his death. Congress adopted the wording to memorialize the first president.

Insidious Changes

Hamilton became the first Secretary of Treasury and proved to be one of the most influential cabinet secretaries of all time.

Born in the West Indies during 1755 or 1757, Hamilton faced early obstacles in his life. At age eight, Hamilton's father left his mother. To further complicate his life, in a time when society had little forgiveness, his parents were not married. As a result, Hamilton could not go to parochial school, and even more challenging, he effectively became an orphan at 13 when his mother died. However, always resilient, Hamilton began working in a shipping company, which he subsequently fully operated by the age of 15. Eventually, a charity collection sent him north to study.

Hamilton attended King's College, where, in 1775, he joined the New York militia and rose to the rank of lieutenant. He joined Washington's staff in 1776, and there he stayed for four years. In February 1781, Hamilton resigned but gained a field command just a few months later in July. He played a significant role in the cavalry during the Colonies' Yorktown victory. Shortly after Yorktown, Hamilton resigned his commission.

In 1782, Hamilton became a New York representative to the Confederation Congress. Already frustrated with the decentralized nature of the American war effort, Hamilton continually worked for an independent source of revenue for the national government. In April 1783, Washington defused a rebellion among officers; however, in June 1783, disgruntled soldiers marched on Philadelphia, and Congress moved to Princeton, New Jersey. Again frustrated, Hamilton resigned Congress in July 1783. In New York, he read law and joined the state bar, helped found the Bank of New York in 1784, and also played a key role in reopening King's College (damaged during fighting in 1776 and closed), which would be renamed Columbia College (now Columbia University). With the US in a financial crisis, Hamilton attended the Annapolis Convention in 1786. Although only five states attended, they agreed to the 1787 Constitutional Convention proposed by Hamilton.

At the Constitutional Convention, Hamilton proposed an elected president and senate to serve for life dependant on good behavior. He drafted a proposal based on national debate incorporating a complex electoral system for these positions. The president would have an absolute veto, and state governors would be by appointment from the federal government. His proposals went nowhere, and although not

~ 51 ~

satisfied with the final draft of the Constitution, he lent his endorsement because it offered a much-needed improvement to the national government. In total, he wrote or helped write, about 50 of the 85 *Federalist Papers*.

As the head of Treasury, Hamilton played a key policy development role. He sought to prepare America's infant financial system for growth in the new age of industry. Hamilton's *Report on Manufactures* proposed:

- protection of emerging American industries (high tariffs);
- physical infrastructure (never fully funded in Antebellum US); and
- financial infrastructure.

Hamilton proposed a broad interpretation of the elastic clause to increase Congressional power over the economy. His *First Report on Public Credit* resulted in the dinner table compromise (with James Madison, brokered by Jefferson), allowing the federal government to assume state debts and placing the new capital on the Potomac River (the District of Columbia).

Hamilton's *Second Report on Public Credit* produced the First Bank of the United States (established in 1791, also the year of a substantial excise tax on liquor resulting in the Whiskey Rebellion). Bonds issued by the bank (paper securities) would increase the money supply allowing for economic growth.

Like Smith, Hamilton believed the future would be won by productivity, and productivity could be greatly enhanced with manufacturing.[26] Although his plan called for government intervention, it did not propose government planning. He did favor increasing the power of the federal government, but mostly as a factor of stability. The government needed to ensure a steady money supply, enhance certain businesses, and get the government's financial house in order. Of course, all this meant money, and taxes are the way for a government to raise money. Enter the whiskey excise tax. The whiskey excise proved to be a substantial domestic test for the infant government.

The whiskey charge proved to be particularly egregious to western farmers for a reason as it, in essence, taxed a farmer's store of wealth. With difficult transport, farmers tended to distill grain not used for

---

[26] Ron Chernow, *Alexander Hamilton*, Penguin Press, 2004, 347, 376-7.

livestock for easy, secure storage and transportation, and as a corollary, the farmers tended to use whiskey as barter in trade. Also, the tax ran at a higher rate for small producers and a lower rate for large producers, nine cents a gallon for small producers, and six cents for large distillers, a truly regressive tax schedule.[27] In all, farmer anger began to foment into more open rebellions, something the Founders had hoped to overcome with the Constitution.

The first armed resistance occurred in Pennsylvania (near Pittsburgh). Tom the Tinker extended the struggle beyond the tax collectors and those who supported them (such as renting offices) to those paying the tax. The tactic of intimidation gained momentum.

In Pennsylvania and Virginia, Washington raised a militia force nearly the size of the Continental Army. When the armed federal force led by Washington, Hamilton, and General Henry "Light-Horse Harry" Lee reached western Pennsylvania in 1794, the rebels had dispersed. Proving themselves difficult to find, eventually, two were sentenced to death (Washington commuted their sentences), two were jailed (one dying before being released), and several were fined.

## THOMAS JEFFERSON AND THE DEMOCRATIC-REPUBLICANS

*The Federalists sought more central authority, but many Americans proved to be skeptical of the new government. Thomas Jefferson became their champion and formed an opposition to the Federalists, specifically Hamilton, even as he served in Washington's cabinet. Eventually, the Democratic-Republicans would coalesce around Jefferson and gain control from the Federalists.*

The Founders agreed on many things, but they also held their perspectives and fears as revealed in the constitutional ratification process. Thomas Jefferson mostly muted during the ratification process, philosophically came down on the side of the Anti-Federalists. Always skeptical of government's door to power and the

---

[27] In economic language, a regressive tax places a disproportionate burden on the poor, a progressive tax slides more of the burden up the ladder to the wealthier population.

Insidious Changes

corruption of tyranny, Jefferson could live with enumerated powers, and a limited government always held in check internally and externally by the states. As the essential Founder, and always seeking consensus, Washington invited Jefferson into his first government under the Constitution. Secretary of State seemed a natural fit as Jefferson had many ties to America's first ally France. However, as much as Washington might have wished for peace and harmony among the Founders, this proved elusive.

Jefferson served Virginia both militarily and politically before becoming the major author of the Declaration of Independence. In the Confederation Congress, he wrote the Land Ordinance of 1784, which laid the groundwork for eastern states to discontinue their claims on western lands, provided provisions for dividing this territory into new states accepted on an equal basis, and prohibited slavery in the new territory. The last provision did not initially pass Congress, but eventually would be adopted in the Northwest Ordinance of 1787. Congress then appointed Jefferson to a diplomatic role joining Benjamin Franklin and John Adams. When Washington became the first president, he reached out to Jefferson to head up the new Department of State, and Jefferson returned home.

Jefferson and Hamilton disagreed on many fronts, with the first having emerged over the national debt and a national capitol. Hamilton nearly gave up his plan to financially organize America by including state war debt, but the eventual dinner table bargain of Jefferson and Hamilton placed the new nation on the road to financial stability and formalized the new capitol of the District of Columbia.[28] In reality, the deal worked extremely well for Jefferson down the road as it allowed the US to borrow money for the Louisiana Purchase and the War of 1812. However, Jefferson remained opposed to big banks and big money, to such a point that when he left Washington's cabinet, the first president never spoke to him again.

Jefferson left the Department of State at the end of 1793 but returned to the federal government as vice-president in 1797 after the fall election of the previous year. Although Jefferson had urged

---

[28] The Compromise of 1790 resulted in the Residence Act for establishing the District of Columbia, and the Assumption Act a month later to consolidate debt. In the final debt consolidation, Jefferson and James Madison successfully negotiated a favorable settlement for their home state of Virginia.

Insidious Changes

Washington to run for reelection, he had little love for the Federalists and despised serving as vice-president under John Adams. Jefferson attempted to undermine diplomatic efforts with the French, resulting in the XYZ Affair, which revealed diplomatic intrigue but backfired on Jefferson, eventually turning American sentiment against the French and resulted in the naval tension, primarily in the Caribbean Sea, of the Quasi-War with the formerly close allies. The Federalists united to pass the Alien and Sedition Acts to restrict the activities of foreign nationals but proved to be split over the issue of war. Ultimately, Jefferson and Democratic-Republicans won the next election, and the Federalists would fade to references in historical footnotes with the exception of one very prominent jurist.

## JOHN MARSHALL, THE SUPREME COURT, CONSTITUTIONAL INTERPRETATION, AND FEDERALISM

*The early political jockeying of the Founders resulted in many precedents. One of the most important of these precedent setters led the Supreme Court from 1801 until his death in 1836. John Marshall's role on the Court would solidify its place in the political institutions of the new nation and remains impactful to this day.*

In history and political science, Chief Justice John Marshall is revered as one of the most, if not the most, important figures in the formative years of the US Supreme Court. The practice of judicial review is credited to Marshall, but his accomplishments were much broader and deeper than even this would suggest. He often solidified the original form of federalism, dual federalism, giving the states considerable police power and limiting the federal government to the authority specifically given in the Constitution.[29] He often acted as a Hamiltonian in that he set the tone for much of our nation's economic policy through the supremacy clause. Yes, states had considerable

---

[29] Police power is defined by Merriam-Webster as well as many other sources to be, ". . . the inherent power of a government to exercise reasonable control over persons and property within its jurisdiction in the interest of the general security, health, safety, morals, and welfare except where legally prohibited." Retrieved from, https://www.merriam-webster.com/dictionary/police%20power.

economic power, but if these proved to conflict with federal law, the federal law prevailed, a specific application of dual federalism. In several groundbreaking cases, the Marshall Court became known for expanding judicial power through constitutional interpretation.

It was the 1803 decision in *Marbury v. Madison,* where Marshall established the principle of judicial review, spelling out the principle in the majority opinion.[30] He followed this up with *Martin v. Hunter's Lessee* (1816), establishing that the Supreme Court had the right to correct interpretations of the US Constitution made by state courts. Both of these decisions provided a foundation for third branch authority, but Marshall also extended Congressional authority through *McCulloch v. Maryland* revolving around the Second Bank of the US.

The Jeffersonians allowed the First Bank of the United States to expire in 1811. However, following the War of 1812, and the resulting inflation, Congress established the Second Bank of the US in 1816. Other Jeffersonians who opposed the national bank placed state taxes on the various branches. Maryland was one of these states, where the head cashier of the Bank of the US branch James McCulloch refused to pay the tax. The importance of the issues moved the case quickly through the state court system to the US Supreme Court.

The McCulloch decision (1819) gave a broad interpretation of the Constitution. The Court upheld the use of the elastic clause ("Let the end be legitimate . . . and all means . . . consistent with the letter and spirit of the Constitution, are constitutional.") to affirm Congressional authority to establish the Bank of the United States. Certainly, Marshall argued, the federal government had enumerated (listed) powers within the Constitution. However, the broad necessary and

---

[30] In the famous Marbury case, William Marbury had been intended as a last-minute appointment of John Adams, but Marbury and others did not receive their official notice before Thomas Jefferson became the new president. Jefferson decided not to make these appointments, and as a result Marbury asked the Court to issue a writ of mandamus to make then Secretary of State James Madison delivery the official documents. Marshall knew he had no mechanism of enforcement, but played his hand well. Citing that Congress had given writ authority through statute but the Constitution had specified only certain areas of original jurisdiction, not including the writ, Marbury did not have the right to petition the Court directly, but rather had to begin in a lower court. As a result, Marshall reduced the immediate power of the Supreme Court but in the long run greatly enhanced it with judicial review or ruling on the constitutionality of Congressional legislation.

proper clause (which Jefferson opposed) allowed Congress to move beyond language to exercise other duties if it supported the legitimate enumerated powers. Finally, Marshall asserted that laws of the federal government, when correctly enacted, were superior to those of the states, the supremacy clause. Despite this decision, the Bank would again expire under the administration of Andrew Jackson (1829-37), but the principle of the elastic clause would long endure.

Another 1819 decision, *Dartmouth College v. Woodward*, solidified the enforcement of contracts. The Massachusetts legislature had made several moves in an attempt to make the private Dartmouth College into a public institution. The school had been organized initially under a charter granted in 1769 by King George III, authorizing its purpose, governing structure, and even land for its operation. The Marshall Court ruled these actions to be a contract with a transfer of private rights, not concessions of a government that could be overtaken by another government. This decision, along with the 1810 decision of *Fletcher v. Peck*, helped solidify the primacy of contracts (the contracts clause) and private property rights over the arbitrary authority of a government. This governmental restraint of authority remained a guiding principle for the Marshall Court in future decisions.

In the 1824 decision of *Gibbons v. Ogden*, Marshall expanded the federal government's regulation of interstate trade by the commerce clause. Because the Constitutional Convention had been convened in large measure as a response to inadequate trade rules between and among states, Marshall held to a broad interpretation of the commerce clause (Congress has the right to regulate trade between and among states). He asserted interstate commerce does not only occur at borders but throughout the transaction, even into the interiors of the various states, a point that has become the single most important instrument of federal power, powerful but not omnipotent. Marshall cautioned that the federal government had no power in commercial transactions that occurred strictly within the boundaries of one state, and he held this concept of dual federalism on a consistent basis. In the 1833 case of *Barron v. Baltimore*, the Court ruled that the Bill of Rights as embodied in the first ten amendments of the US Constitution applied only to the federal government and not to states. Such interpretation led to the later adoption of the 14th Amendment during Reconstruction, which applies the principles of due process

~ 57 ~

and equal protection under the law to states with the federal government as the arbiter. Eventually, the application of the 14th Amendment would play a significant role in ending the first form of federalism, dual federalism.[31]

Throughout Marshall's tenure, he worked very hard to gain a consensus within the Court. Under his tutelage, the Court established early guidance for the operation of federalism and reinforced the basics of private property rights. He also instilled the procedure of issuing a majority opinion with a decision. Before this, each justice issued his own opinion, known as *seriatim* (inherited from the British), but the Marshall approach gave a more unified approach for the third branch.

The infant federal government found a champion in Marshall. Many more cases could be cited, but these represent the essence of the time. Marshall proved to be a strong nationalist who sought to preserve the spirit and foundation of the Union by not overstepping boundaries of authority and retaining the primacy of the individual.

Much of history implies that the Federalists ended with the election and defeat of Adams in the presidential election of 1800. However, a closer look relates a different story. Even a short study of Marshall makes it obvious that the Federalist influence lasted well into the 19th Century and developed the first form of federalism practiced in the US.[32]

## SLAVERY AND THE CIVIL WAR

*The US proved to be divided over the issue of slavery from its*

---

[31] The 1937 decision in *Palko v. Connecticut* (this is a misspelling, the defendant's name was Palka) ruled that double jeopardy protection of the 5th Amendment did not apply to the states. This would be overturned in 1969 with *Benton v. Maryland* that applied the 14th Amendment to double jeopardy.

[32] John Adams appointed a kindred soul in Marshall. Spending the extremely difficult winter of 1778 at Valley Forge, Marshall met George Washington and many other Founders who built America. He gained great admiration for Washington (writing an extensive biography of Washington after the first president's death) and a commitment to the success of the new union embodied in the 1787 constitution. However, his orientation to the Federalist Party kept him busy with the Jeffersonians (of course, the reason for Adams' appointment).

*inception. The tension between free and slave states formed a temporary period of coexistence; however, the Fugitive Slave Laws, Kansas-Nebraska Act, and Dred Scott decision ended the uneasy peace and resulted in armed conflict.*

Moving our time travel forward to 1860, we find the Union in crisis. The regional division of the North and South had grown into a full-on confrontation. John Brown had even taken rebellious action against the federal government in an attempt to force change, but this has not yet occurred. However, the coming election will tell the tale.

Being a Northerner (remember, we moved to New England), and perhaps a Methodist at this time, we oppose slavery. Like many in New England, we will vote for Abraham Lincoln, a Republican opposed to slavery and the spread of slavery, certainly a real concern after Bleeding Kansas.[33] Although Lincoln cannot obtain a popular majority, he will win the Electoral College and become the 16th president of the US. However, the very existence of the Union will be put to the test in the month following his inauguration when South Carolinians took armed action against federal troops at Fort Sumter. Soon, the fate of the republic will be decided by brother vs. brother in a conflict to settle the fate of slavery, and the American Union.

In reality, two nations had existed side-by-side since the beginning of the republic. The issue of slavery philosophically divided the North from the South throughout the antebellum period, and this became divisive on almost every front. As noted, this began during the fight for independence and continued to the 1787 convention, which produced the Three-fifths Compromise. The compromise allowed slaves to be counted as three-fifths a person for representation purposes (in the House of Representatives). The effect under law was that slaves were at least part of a citizen, but this would change as the US increasingly drifted into a separation of North and South.

Slavery long had been a part of the human condition. However, the Founders struggled with this reality, and even slaveholders such as

---

[33] The Kansas-Nebraska Act of 1854 offered the ability of new states to vote on their status as free or slave states. As Kansas solidified plans to enter the Union, slave state neighbor Missouri proved to be a launching point for pro-slavery antagonists. The tension resulted in several raids and deaths before Kansas gained statehood as a free state.

~ 59 ~

Jefferson had problems with the practice. In the end, to keep the states united, it had to be accepted by those with doubts. Those doubts remained, even to the point of allowing the Confederate Congress to prohibit the practice in the Northwest Territories. However, it would be long after the demise of the Articles of Confederation before the problem of slavery would be solved. The story of Dred Scott provides a telling insight into the conflict of slavery practice and the foundation of America.

The Three-fifths Compromise gave slaves some standing within the Constitution. However, a lot of uncertainty as to what that standing actually represented took years to sort out. In the end, the Dred Scott Decision of the 1840-50s placed black slaves into a position of not being recognized under the law other than as chattel (personal property).

Although we often hear of the Missouri Compromise (no more slave states above the southern border of Missouri), the second Missouri Compromise is often forgotten. The original Missouri state constitution contained a clause that restricted free blacks, or mixed black/white heritage, from residing in the state. To push the act through, Henry Clay added a provision to the bill stating that this clause did not intrude upon the rights of US citizens. The language appeared to put the issue to rest, but the definition of citizenship remained in limbo concerning free blacks.

Army surgeon, Dr. John Emerson, moved from Missouri to free states, taking along the enslaved Dred Scott. In Wisconsin, Scott took a wife, a civil action not allowed to him in Missouri. As Emerson moved around, Scott also moved around and worked for other people, always hired out by Emerson. Finally, Scott returned with the family to Missouri. After the sudden death of the surgeon, Scott tried to purchase his freedom from Mrs. Emerson. She refused, so a subsequent lawsuit sought his freedom.

The Dred Scott case went all the way to the US Supreme Court, where the Taney justices ruled that moving to a free state did not free a slave. The first case began in 1846, taking two trials for Scott to be declared free. However, the Missouri Supreme Court ruled, in opposition to previous decisions, that Scott was not a citizen (not free). On appeal, the US Supreme Court ruled that with the Missouri decision, Scott was not a citizen, and therefore, the Court had no grounds to hear the case. The Dred Scott ruling of 1857 added fuel to

Insidious Changes

the condition of free/slave state tension as did Harriet Beecher Stowe's novel, *Uncle Tom's Cabin*, written in opposition to the second Fugitive Law and a significant piece of literature in favor of abolition.[34]

Under the Compromise of 1850, Congress had skirted a crisis in the short-run. The five laws involved:

1. admission of California as a free state;
2. the New Mexico territory made no prohibition of slavery;
3. Texas was compensated for relinquishing claims to the west (it had already joined the Union in 1845 as a slave state);
4. the Fugitive Slave Law required that free state residents would return escaped and captured slaves; and
5. eliminated slave trafficking in Washington, DC, but slavery remained intact.

The Kansas-Nebraska Act followed in 1854, which allowed the residents of these territories to decide if they would accept or reject slavery. However, tension soon reached a boiling point.

The Border War began as Missouri slaveholders sought to eliminate the possibility of a next-door refuge for runaway slaves. The dispute raged for the remainder of the decade: in a sense, the Civil War had already begun. Congress proposed admission of Kansas under the Lecompton Constitution, but with a second referendum, the voters of Kansas rejected the document that made no mention of slavery. The situation tore the Democrat Party in two and allowed Abraham Lincoln to gain the presidency as a Republican in the 1860 election. A full-fledged war would soon erupt.[35]

In December 1860, before Abraham Lincoln could be sworn in as president, South Carolina seceded from the Union. Before Lincoln's inauguration on March 4, 1861, six other states had joined the original rebel. Finally, on April 12, shots rang out at Fort Sumter, and the American Civil War began. Quickly, the Confederates won at Bull Run, Virginia, as they would win the second battle there the following year. These battles were part of the eventful year of 1862, which included battles at Shiloh, Second Bull Run, and Antietam

---

[34] Will Kaufman, *The Civil War in American Culture*, Edinburgh University Press, 2006, 18.

[35] Kansas would be admitted as a free state in 1861, Nebraska became a state in 1867.

Insidious Changes

(Sharpsburg). In 1863, the Battle of Gettysburg and the Siege of Vicksburg proved to be turning points for a Union victory. Lincoln issued the Emancipation Proclamation, laying the groundwork for abolition contained in the 13th Amendment. West Virginia broke away from Virginia and became the 35th state. The following year proved to be decisive.

In 1864, Union forces pursued a successful campaign in Virginia. Sherman conducted his "March to the Sea" in Georgia, leaving total destruction in a wide path. Union control of Vicksburg, Mississippi, Texas, Arkansas, and Louisiana, as well as their resources, were cut off from the rest of the Confederacy. Finally, Lincoln won reelection as president. The fighting ended the next year when, on April 9, 1865, the war officially ended when Lee surrendered to Grant at the Appomattox Court House in Virginia. However, the victor would not long enjoy the triumph of the Union as John Wilkes Booth would assassinate Lincoln.

## LINCOLN'S LEGACY

*The modern concept of political freedom is associated with Abraham Lincoln as much as with any other person in history. His resistance to secession and slavery, the Emancipation Proclamation which led to the end of slavery with the 13th Amendment, and the Gettysburg Address, a timeless statement of unity and self-government, all made Lincoln a legendary and revered president. Today, he is still considered one of the most important presidents challenged only by Washington, who provided the founding cornerstone for our country.*

*Historian Eric Foner considers the 13th, 14th, and 15th Amendments to be the second founding of the country, opening liberty, rights, and freedom for all citizens. Certainly, Lincoln set the groundwork for these impactful amendments that, whether they were the second founding or the logical extension of the founding, continue to shape the American ideal of liberty, freedom, and equality.*

As president, Lincoln worked hard to preserve the Union and shape its future. At Gettysburg, he delivered the tone that would become the national morality for the conclusion of the war by appealing to a higher power. Of course, the Founders had also

~ 62 ~

appealed to a higher authority, that the Creator endowed all men with perfect freedom and that government is instituted to protect that freedom. Also, as we know, they could not perfectly establish this ideal because of the South's attachment to a hierarchical society which included slavery. This mission to include all in under the umbrella of freedom and release them from the bondage of slavery became Lincoln's crusade as the Civil War ground on through his first term in the White House. It was a noble and religious mission, as expressed in the "Battle Hymn of the Republic." Appearing with the February publication of the Atlantic Monthly in 1862, Julia Ward Howe's lyrics solidified the march to freedom by the North, a mission that left little ground for compromise. Lincoln would continue with this righteous theme throughout the remaining conflict.

At Gettysburg, Lincoln delivered one of the most compelling speeches in American history. He vowed that government "of the people, by the people, and for the people" would not disappear from human history. With this simple speech, with the powerful words of the Preamble of the Constitution, the North expressed its meaning of the war and sought an end that would be decisive. The Emancipation Proclamation clearly outlined Lincoln's intent to end human bondage, as would occur with the ratification of the 13th Amendment in 1863.

The war did end slavery; however, the slave states found various ways to circumvent equality. Black Codes were passed in several states, to distinguish between free blacks and whites. The Ku Klux Klan, originally formed in Tennessee, became a mechanism of social control by whites over blacks. Eventually, two Reconstruction amendments were added to the Constitution to bolster the newly established rights of former slaves:

14th A person born in the US is a citizen (specifically allowed former slaves and their offspring to be citizens); due process and equal protection applied to the states

15th Right to vote for all male citizens of age

The vision of Radical Republicans to transform the South, expressed in the three amendments of this First Civil Rights Era, persisted for years. Former slaves served in Congress, and the federal government did desegregate to employ the new citizens. However, all of this came in the face of resistance, and finally, the reformers gave way to weariness. The assassination of Lincoln, the opposition of the Ku Klux Klan, Black Codes, and other methods kept a tiered Southern system based on race.  Reconstruction officially ended in 1877 with the election compromise that made Rutherford B. Hayes president. All Southern states returned as full members of the Union again, and life continued somewhat modified, but not fundamentally changed for another eight decades.

One final note: the 15th Amendment completed the expansion of voting rights to include black males, whether born a slave or free.  It did not include women, white or black, or Native American Indians. However, the hard-won precedent had been set: the Declaration of Independence did not exclude a group based on race or skin color. However, the full practice of expanded political liberty would take many more years to evolve, but it did happen, and in no small part because of the path pursued by Lincoln.

Insidious Changes

# V: EMERGENCE OF THE PROGRESSIVE

## DEFINING THE PROGRESSIVE ERA

*Constitutional reform from a limited role of government to an expanded concept and practice of government at the federal level might be the most succinct definition of the Progressive Era. Almost all reforms ushered in the era of the expert developing and implementing policy, along with the expansion of the bureaucratic state. Finally, during the New Deal, the groundwork would be laid for a new relationship between the federal government and all US citizens. The states became secondary, as Washington, DC, grew in size and authority.*

Our next stop in time travel takes us to 1910. Here we encounter a world very different from anything we have seen before. First off, the internal combustion engine has arrived! Automobiles are starting to make an appearance on the American scene. Cars join trains as methods of transportation, and even tractors operate in farm fields here and there. Electricity powers the large and growing cities.

The 1910 census would be the last showing the US as a rural country. From 1920 on, more Americans lived in cities than on the farm, and no wonder as industrialization grew in the urban areas that offered such amenities as electricity, mass transit (light trains and cable cars), housing for the masses needed in factory work at the time, and of course, access to rail. The world changed dramatically after the Civil War, and with these changes, some Americans began to question the role of government. Should it be more active? Should government be a proactive problem-solver rather than the dispenser of justice? With the dawn of a new century, questions and reform came.

The Founders of America sought to limit the power of government, believing the threat of too much government far outweighed its benefits. The Founders' belief held throughout most of the 19th Century, but nothing lasts forever. After the Civil War, doubters of the primary founding principle of limited government began to emerge as American urban areas rapidly developed, laying the foundations of a new political movement. Reconstruction had

Insidious Changes

provided for the federal government to be involved in state government through the 14<sup>th</sup> Amendment. Also, technology provided the basis for federal regulation of economic activity. The Progressives, as they became known, believed the government should take an active role in society, and with tools and rationale in place, government programs began to expand.

We can roughly identify the Progressive Era from 1890 through 1920. However, elements of the movement began even earlier and have persisted, very much influencing American politics today, an era marked by political and social activism.[36] The *laissez-faire* approach to government and the economy gave way to a drive for governmental activism and economic regulation resulting in several changes, and ultimately, in the federal government becoming an integral part of every citizen's daily life.

In the early 20<sup>th</sup> Century, Robert La Follette (1855-1925) of Wisconsin introduced the Wisconsin Idea into politics and formed the National Progressive Republican League (1911). La Follette made a key assertion that expert research and input should accompany legislation. His policy reforms included the initiative, referendum, recall, direct primaries, workers compensation, minimum wage, progressive taxation, and women's suffrage (his wife, Belle Case, was a suffragette).

Wholesale changes regarding the practice of federalism became commonplace and institutionalized in this early period. The 16<sup>th</sup>, 17<sup>th</sup>, and even the 18<sup>th</sup> Amendments all expanded federal authority. Other reforms, such as the establishment of the Federal Reserve System as the national bank, went through the route of legislation rather than amendments. Still, the result proved the same, more federal authority. As the Progressives moved their agenda, the federal government grew in all aspects. Some of this governmental expansion came from necessity, such as railroad uniformity, some came with an express purpose (16<sup>th</sup> and 17<sup>th</sup> Amendments). What were once local issues now became national issues. Along with technology and politics, urbanization and war also played significant factors in governmental expansion.

---

[36] Even religion got into the movement with Jacob Riis' 1890 publication of *How the Other Half Lives: Studies Among the Tenements of New York* and Walter Rauschenbusch's 1907 text, *Christianity and the Social Crisis*.

Insidious Changes

The Progressive Era was certainly the kickoff period of big government: a lot of the impetus came from cities where people viewed (and view) government as an everyday part of life. Place this in contrast to rural folk who tend to like government at a distance. As the nation became more technologically advanced, it became more urbanized. As the US population grew more urbanized, the more government they accepted. Modern warfare also stimulated the growth of government with its demands on the organization of production to manufacture large quantities of weapons. These trends, along with the instability of market cycles, increased the demands put on government, and the Progressives were more than happy to comply, especially at the federal level.

## THE PROGRESSIVE ERA AS TRANSFORMATIONAL

*Several reform movements that came together around the beginning of the 20th Century are considered part of the Progressive Era. All of these reform movements resulted in significant changes to our constitutional system. Almost all of these changes left an imprint of the expanding authority of the federal government. The expansion of federal authority certainly qualifies as a departure from the Founders' limited government principles, but very few fundamental changes utilized the amendment process. Instead, the preferred methods of transformation were Congressional regulation and Court interpretation.*

We will notice during this stop in our time travel that government is expanding. As noted above, technology proved to be a driving force in some of this, but growth also resulted from purposeful political design. With the US growing as a global power, the perception of needed centralization of power to compete on the world stage also grew. So, with plenty of federal authority advocates to be found, the Progressive movement found fertile ground for the expansion of federal authority as well as increasing professional expertise. This bias for "professionalism" expanded the regulatory state that Progressives considered essential for modern governing.

Government economic regulation began with *Munn v. Illinois* and the establishment of the Interstate Commerce Commission (ICC).[37]

Insidious Changes

In the Munn decision, the Court ruled that Congress does indeed have the ability to regulate interstate commerce. The case, brought by the Illinois legislature's response to the National Grange's push for rail rate regulations (the farmers' organization that supported government regulation of rail rates), permanently placed the federal government in the business regulation industry.[38] Although several cases after Munn provided restrictive parameters on this power, the precedent had been placed in motion. In the 1890 decision of *Chicago, Milwaukee and St. Paul v. Minnesota*, the Court laid down the idea of substantive due process. Due process had been a key factor in Munn's challenge (the defense complained that the warehouse's right to store and move grain had been removed by government action without the company's input), but this 1890 case resolved that legal issue: if the regulation is deemed reasonable by the judiciary, the bar of *substantive* due process had been met.

Injunction became a tool with the Pullman Strike of 1894. When Eugene V. Debs of the American Railway Union enticed the workers of Pullman Palace Car Company (the famous Pullman cars of the time) to strike, much of the transportation system in the Midwest ground to a halt. With 125,000 workers on the sidelines, President Grover Cleveland's administration, based on the disruption of mail deliveries (a lot of mail moved over the rails at the time), went to court seeking to end the work stoppage. Given an injunction, the president sent federal troops to resume railroad operations. However, the resulting riots destroyed a rail yard and ended with 30 dead. In the end, the Pullman Strike would fail.[39]

Although careful at first, the Court continued to expand the regulatory power of the federal government. In *Swift v. US* (1905), the justices decided that Congress could regulate anything that *might*

---

[37] Congress passed the Interstate Commerce Act in 1887 to establish the Interstate Commerce Commission, the first independent regulatory agency to begin building the fourth branch of government, the administrative state. The initial charge to the ICC involved making rates reasonable and even-handed. Its authority expanded over time until Congress began a deregulation movement across government, eventually abolishing the agency in 1995.

[38] Although the Court could only rule on Congressional ability to regulate interstate commerce, the Munn decision allowed states to regulate economic activity if these regulations did not impede the enumerated power of Congress.

[39] Labor Day would be added as a national holiday in remembrance of those who died in the strike.

Insidious Changes

become a part of interstate commerce (this would even be extended to intrastate commerce that "in the aggregate" might influence interstate trade in the 1942 Wickard decision). The final nail of this period came with *US v. Grimaud* (1911), a decision that gave regulations the force of law – Congress did not need to enact the regulation, they could delegate the authority! This authority to delegate became the basis of the administrative state.

So, in the watershed year of 1877, Congress enacted the legislation to form the ICC. The commission initially sought to standardize railway delivery and operation. Consisting of five members appointed by the president, and serving with senatorial confirmation, the body became the first independent regulatory agency and the foundation of the fourth branch of government, the administrative/regulatory bureaucracy. Progressives had their foothold for the idea of appointed "experts" transforming the American constitutional system from accountable, elected officials, especially in Congress, to the more insulated appointed personnel. Throughout this process, the definitive change mechanism of amendments fell into little, if any, consideration. Black robe change became common, but not exclusive.

During the Progressive Era, activist presidents also appeared. Although most presidents have pushed their authority at times, Theodore Roosevelt proved to be one of the most effective at this game. With little doubt, TR could take a job and define it in his terms, and like all his exploits, TR took on the presidency with vigor unmatched by his rivals.

During the early 20th Century, TR reinterpreted the Constitution from a document of enumerated (listed) powers to one of prohibition: if not strictly prohibited, the power is available. Being prone to accept the idea of progress (science and technology improve society), he established the Bureau of Reclamation, eventually leading to the construction of Hoover Dam and Glen Canyon Dam to irrigate western lands. He outmaneuvered Congress to establish 16 million acres of national forest. Like John Muir, the founder of the Sierra Club, TR believed in the enjoyment of nature; unlike Muir, however, TR also believed in the use of natural resources for human benefit. As a result, he believed in government control over much of the land in the West, and public projects to exploit its usefulness. However,

TR did not stop his governmental expansion with his transformation of the West.

Roosevelt pushed a larger, more active government, and he took on big business in a big way. The Hepburn Act (1906) allowed the Interstate Commerce Commission (1887) to establish maximum rail rates, which came in response to challenges of the enforcement authority to the ICC's ability to regulate rates. (The initial rationale, promoted by the Grange movement, was to eliminate the discriminatory practices of rail charges giving volume discounts to big shippers and charging higher rates to low-volume farmers.) He used the Sherman Anti-Trust Act to break up the Northern Securities Company, a move upheld by the Supreme Court (*Northern Securities v. US*). His administration oversaw the passage of the Meat Inspection Act and the Pure Food and Drug Act (came about in reaction to Upton Sinclair's book *The Jungle*). He called his policies the Square Deal, designed to make the economic playing field level for all participants. However, despite the massive force of TR, change came not only from political desire but also from circumstance.

Economic upheaval also spurred the growth of government regulation. The demise of the Knickerbocker Trust in New York triggered the Panic of 1907. Although J. P. Morgan bailed out the financial establishment, the ensuing recession lasted a year, leading directly to the legislation that eventually formed the Federal Reserve System. After a visit to Europe, Rhode Island Senator Nelson Aldrich returned home with a notion that the government must establish a central banking system and proposed legislation to that effect (superimposing European models that the Founders had rejected). The Aldrich Plan initially met resistance from Western states and farmers who viewed it as a sellout to the Eastern financial establishment. The 1912 victory of Congressional and presidential Democrats seemed to spell doom to the plan, but with a few modifications, Woodrow Wilson and the Democrats of Congress passed the Federal Reserve Act establishing 12 regional banks and the Board of Governors to provide financial stability for the country.

So, in 1913, the Federal Reserve System came into existence to stabilize the country's money supply.[40] Also, that year the

---

[40] Since 1913 the Federal Reserve has gained several other responsibilities including

Insidious Changes

Underwood tariff reduced the tariff amount (the 16th Amendment establishing income tax would help replace this lost revenue). The Clayton Anti-Trust Act further restricted anti-competitive practices (this law included treble damage awards as well as injunctive relief in lawsuits).[41]

Despite the Sherman Anti-Trust Act and the Northern Securities decision, business found a mostly reliable friend in the Supreme Court. In *Lochner v. New York* (1905), the Court ruled that state government could not interfere with a private contract between employer and employee. The Lochner case revolved around a New York law limiting bakery hours. The Court cited the due process clause of the 14th Amendment as barring state legislatures from regulating interstate commerce, a ruling that stood 32 years (in 1937 *West Coast Hotel v. Parrish* allowed statutes to address socio-economic conditions). However, the always active Progressives in executive and legislative roles were not to be denied: they would pass more amendments in this period than any other era since the adoption of the Bill of Rights.

The 16th Amendment gave the country income taxes after the Court struck down the previous income tax provision in *Pollock v. Farmers' Loan and Trust Company.* The Pollock decision upheld the constitutional provision that taxes would be apportioned to the states based on population, defeating one purpose of tax, placing a more relative burden on the rich than the poor. With the ratification of the amendment in 1913, and the passage of the Revenue Act of that year, a graduated scale of taxing income (the higher levels pay more) began its permanent run.

The dramatic constitutional changes continued with the adoption of the 17th Amendment, which resulted in the direct election of US senators. Quickly the state legislatures demonstrated their willingness to give up power. The original design, having the people choose their representatives through direct election and senators chosen to represent the states through selection by the state legislators, would be replaced in less than a year! The Progressives argued this would fight

---

maintaining high levels of employment. Today, there is often reference to the dual mission of the Reserve, low inflation and high employment.

[41] The Sherman Act did not outlaw monopolies; instead, it targeted business trusts that throttled competition allowing these companies to deliberately and "unnaturally" control markets.

Insidious Changes

corruption (elected state officials being bribed and playing partisan politics), but it also completely changed the nature of checks and balances: states as unique entities lost their representation in the US government. The result would be another blow in the diminishing stature of dual federalism.

The 18th Amendment gave us Prohibition on the federal level along with a resulting black market and a lesson in banning certain vices (the 21st Amendment in 1933 repealed Prohibition and recovered alcohol excise tax for the federal government).

## WORLD WAR AND GOVERNING IN AMERICA

*Government planning and expansion received a boost from the Great War (World War I) as the Progressive Era drew to a close. Total war brought the federal government newly practiced authority over industrial production and civil liberties. The war also propelled the US to great power status internationally, but Americans would prove reluctant to pick up the responsibilities traditionally associated with such status.*

Total war exploded in 1914. Technically neutral from 1914 into 1917, the US provided the Allies, especially Britain and France, with financial and material support. Seeking a second term, Woodrow Wilson's slogan, "He kept us out of war," proved successful. However, it was not far into Wilson's second term that the American Doughboy would enter the fray.

Germany continually questioned American neutrality: the sinking of the *Lusitania*, the Zimmermann Telegram, and Germany's unrestricted submarine warfare eventually brought America closer to armed participation. Wilson did try to broker a peace, but the attempt failed. Finally, as the German submarines became more aggressive, Wilson convinced Congress to, as is often stated when discussing US objectives in World War I, "make the world safe for democracy," and America officially declared war in April 1917.[42]

---

[42] "Joint Address to Congress Leading to Declaration of War Against Germany," retrieved from http://www.ourdocuments.gov/doc.php?doc=61&page=transcript.

The prosecution of total war grew the federal bureaucracy as victory depended on the coordination of manufactured goods: processed foods, machine guns, ammunition, tanks, etc. The "Doughboys" needed everything, and the American industrial machine could easily provide these necessities.

The War Industries Board (numerous other boards assisted it, but this board held the most far-reaching power) coordinated mass production and pushed for the standardization of parts. The increased demand for goods caused labor agitation for higher wages and the threat of strikes (the Board did exert its influence to increase wages and avoid disruption of production). In existence from 1916 until 1919, the Board oversaw an increase of industrial production in the neighborhood of 37 percent. Gross national product (GNP) rose 60 percent during this period and 85 percent into 1920.

The production of the war necessities turned the US from a net debtor into a net creditor. Another significant change came with the Great Migration as black sharecroppers moved from Southern cotton fields to Northern factories. Also, increasing numbers of women went to work. Conscription (the draft) also became a part of the war machine. An army of 200,000 increased to 4.7 million and sent over two million troops to Europe, with about 1.4 million seeing combat action. The Sedition Act suppressed opposition at home (with the First Red Scare following the war, Socialist Eugene V. Debs would be imprisoned, and there received nearly a million votes for president). Truly, American government and society changed with total war.

During the Revolutionary War and the Civil War, the US government had printed money (Continentals and Greenbacks, respectively) to finance the fighting. During World War I, the War Revenue Act took advantage of the new income tax to support the war effort. Congress went after the super-rich increasing tax rates on those with incomes of a $1,000,000-plus from 10.3 to 70.3 percent. Despite this huge increase in income tax rates, the federal government well outspent this source of revenue: in the end, about 58 percent of the total 32.9 billion spent on the war came from borrowing.[43] The Liberty Bonds and eventually Victory Bonds emerged to help overcome the shortfall.

---

[43] "US Economy in World War I," retrieved from http://eh.net/encyclopedia/u-s-economy-in-world-war-i/.

Insidious Changes

The massive infusion of American troops and material into Europe finally tipped the scale in favor of the Allies, despite the Bolshevik (Communist) Revolution and withdrawal of Russia from the fighting under the Treaty of Brest-Livtosk. In the end, Wilson set forth an ambitious plan to curtail such massive future confrontations with his Fourteen Points speech in 1918. The speech called for openness between and among nations, free trade, self-determination (hoping for democracy), as well as an international body to foster cooperation among nations, the League of Nations, a defense pact with other nations which would be a real departure from Washington's warnings if enacted.

Despite a tremendous effort, Wilson's presidency ended on a low note. He struggled with the vindictive French President Georges Clemenceau, eventually abandoning most of his Fourteen Points to gain the League of Nations. The Treaty of Versailles included reparations (which would wreak havoc with the German economy), the territorial gains of the Treaty of Brest-Livtosk were negated, and all colonial possessions of Germany were confiscated. As bad as all this may seem, it became even worse when Wilson returned to the US.

Back home, Wilson went head-to-head with Senator Henry Cabot Lodge. In no mood to compromise again, Wilson took to a national tour seeking to win over public opinion and put pressure on Congress. On this trip, he suffered a stroke, and his presidency declined. His wife Edith and his personal physician, Dr. Cary Grayson, interacted with Wilson at the time. They screened all visitors, which certainly could not have improved the chances of adopting the treaty terms. In the midst of this tension, the Spanish Flu, demobilization from the war, and the Red Scare would hit the US. In the end, with the treaty ratification failing (the US would be a League of Nations observer, not a member), Wilson's legacy closed on a somber note.

Despite his failure to completely implement his vision of international cooperation, Wilson's foreign policy stated in his Fourteen Points remains a fixture in American diplomacy. Self-determination, democracy, collective security, and international law have remained as goals of the idealists, making American foreign policy (on the other hand, realists are concerned with keeping American power as the most effective tool of foreign policy).

# THE CHANGING STATUS OF WOMEN DURING THE PROGRESSIVE ERA

*In 1920, after years of attempts, the ratification of the 19th Amendment gave women the vote in federal elections.*

After years of struggle, the 19th Amendment allowed women to vote in federal elections.  Shortly after the American Revolution, Mary Wollstonecraft argued that women were not inherently inferior to men but rather less educated, which made them appear to be inferior (*A Vindication of the Rights of Women*, 1792).  Wollstonecraft challenged many conventions of her time, and as a result, her thoughts were mostly overlooked until the feminist movement of the late 20th Century.[44]  However, Wollstonecraft would not be the only voice for women.  The much more conventional Abigail Adams famously appealed to her husband John while he served in the Second Continental Congress during March 1776, "remember the ladies and be more generous and favorable to them than your ancestors. Do not put such unlimited power into the hands of the Husbands . . . If . . . not . . . we are determined to foment a Rebellion, and will not hold ourselves bound by any Laws in which we have no voice or Representation." Despite the eloquent appeal, women would not gain the vote during the Revolution and only after a protracted struggle.

The year 1848 is often cited as the beginning push that eventually resulted in women's suffrage.  Also, this is the year that Elizabeth Cady Stanton wrote the Declarations of Sentiments and presented the document to the gathering of women rights activists at Seneca Falls, NY.  The document, based on the Declaration of Independence, is now considered a seminal statement in the successful push for women's suffrage, but even with this effort, nearly a century passed before the issues of the convention would be addressed in public policy.

---

[44] Wollstonecraft died in 1797 after the birth of her second daughter Mary Shelley who would later write the classic novel *Frankenstein*.  Wollstonecraft's husband, William Godwin also a writer and philosopher, would posthumously publish her *Memoirs* in 1798 revealing her disdain for convention and setting back her personal reputation for years.

Insidious Changes

During the 1850s, the women's movement formed a strong bond with the Abolitionists. The Civil War put women's suffrage on the backburner, but it quickly revived under the guidance of Stanton, Susan B. Anthony, and their American Equal Rights Association, soon to be replaced by the National Woman Suffrage Association. In the Wyoming Territory, women first gained the right to vote in 1869, but the movement gained little momentum from the breakout legislation. Lucy Stone also revived the movement with the American Woman Suffrage Association, which published the *Woman's Journal*.

The emergence of the Women's Christian Temperance Union in 1874 put a new twist on the suffrage movement. Their political strength made the liquor industry nervous, and probably with good reason: if women got the vote, which the WCTU supported, they could have the strength to outlaw the production and sale of spirits! The 1890 merger of the NWSA and AWSA placed Susan B. Anthony, in front of the suffrage forces resulting in a switch of focus from Capitol Hill to the statehouses. First, as a territory and then as a state, Wyoming embraced voting for women, Colorado would follow suit in 1893, along with Utah and Idaho in 1896.[45] The American Federation of Labor would join the suffrage backers along with the Women's Trade Union League of New York to join shortly thereafter.

Several states adopted women's suffrage in the early 20th Century, and even a national party, TR's Bull Moose Party, took up the cause. In 1914, the General Federation of Women's Clubs also joined the movement. Finally, with the election of Jeannette Rankin as representative from Montana, the Democrat Party adopted women's suffrage. Wilson lobbied a reluctant Senate, and in 1919 the 19th Amendment went to the states for ratification (it would be ratified the next year).

## THE CHANGING STATUS OF MINORITIES IN THE PROGRESSIVE ERA

---

[45] Wyoming territory under Governor John Allen Campbell gave women the right to vote in 1869 and this remained as it joined the Union in 1890. Wyoming is home to many female firsts and is officially nicknamed the "Equality State."

Insidious Changes

*The status of black Americans deteriorated throughout the Progressive Era. The American Indian Citizenship Act made Native Americans citizens with voting rights in 1924.*

As women pushed for their place in the American political arena, blacks struggled with their position in American society. The Fuller Court had placed blacks in the back of the bus, literally, in *Plessy v. Ferguson*. The Plessy precedent set the standard of "separate but equal" for six decades. The Fuller Court also, interestingly enough, living in America, citing that the 14th Amendment was intended for and should be applied only to freed black slaves. Within this framework of issues, blacks became more dissatisfied, faced a major setback, and began to organize for change.

In 1896, the Court under Melville Fuller heard a case from Louisiana concerning public transportation. Homer Plessy had been arrested in a train car marked "Whites Only" and being partially black, the law did not allow him in the car. The Fuller court ruled that "separate but equal" accommodations were allowed under the Constitution, and Jim Crow laws became the way of the land until 1954. The only dissenting vote from John Marshall Harlan carried the comment, "The Constitution is color blind, and neither knows nor tolerates classes among citizens." A setback to civil rights, the black community struggled to define an appropriate strategy to counter their second-class status.

Before the Plessy decision, Booker T. Washington (1856-1915) had already delivered his Atlanta Address (1895). Washington called for cooperation with whites to elevate the black situation through thrift and industry. His work, *Up from Slavery,* continues to be cited as essential to understanding the African-American experience. However, not all blacks agreed with Washington. Activist W.E.B. Du Bois, along with fellow reformists, retreated to the Canadian side of Niagara Falls during the summer of 1905. They emerged with a statement of principles that supported the deliberate elimination of racial segregation in the US, and the promotion of economic, social, legal equality for blacks. The movement eventually merged with a group of reformist whites in 1911 to form the National Association for the Advancement of Colored People. Much like the women's movement, changes for blacks would take several decades to find

Insidious Changes

fertile ground. Somewhat ironically, and as mentioned above, total war spurred the economic advancement of blacks and their migration from the rural South to the industrial North.

Although economic opportunity seemed to result from global war, the Progressive Era did not politically advance the black population. President Wilson would fully segregate the federal government, and black workers were generally locked out of skilled labor and labor unions. The Mann Act (1910) intended to fight sex slave trafficking, would be used against heavyweight boxing champion Jack Jackson while traveling with his white girlfriend (later they were married). He would not be pardoned until the presidency of Donald Trump. In the 1920s, the Ku Klux Klan, which flourished during Southern Reconstruction, exploded in a resurgence that even penetrated some northern states. Although the legal status of blacks in the South remained entrenched and legal equality remained elusive, Native American Indians underwent a dramatic official change.

Under the 1787 Constitution, tribal Americans were considered semi-independent nations and not under the jurisdiction of the US other than direction expressly passed through Congress. As a result, the 14th Amendment specified those not subject to the jurisdiction of the United States when it came to citizenship. In 1871, the Dawes Act divided some tribal land up to be taken by individual members of the specified tribe, or by white settlers. This became a decisive factor in the statehood of Oklahoma. However, tribal status changed during the Coolidge administration.

In 1924, the American Indian Citizenship Act made the Native Americans citizens with voting rights and appropriation for representation in the House of Representatives. Finally, the Indian Reorganization Act of 1934 is considered the legal standing for tribal council jurisdiction on reservations. Some constitutional rights extensions were provided in Public Law 280 passed by Congress in 1953. Subsequent court decisions have clarified tribal jurisdiction over members and to the exclusion of non-tribal persons.

## SIGNIFICANT PROGRESSIVE ERAFREE SPEECH DECISIONS

*Some crucial decisions concerning political free speech occurred in the early decades of the 20th Century. Justice Oliver Holmes, Jr. would give us the phrase "clear and present danger" when providing a test on speech and suggesting limits on free speech. In a later case, the Near decision would provide journalists with a wide berth concerning their ability to publish political information.*

With the triumph of Bolsheviks in Russia (which became the Union of Soviet Socialist Republics in 1922) the fear of communism and socialism grew in the US. On January 2, 1919, Attorney General A. Mitchell Palmer, with J. Edgar Hoover executing orders on the ground, began the Red Scare with his evening raids. This era would launch the Sacco and Vanzetti epic: two Italian-born anarchists arrested in 1920, convicted of robbery and murder in 1921, and eventually executed in 1927. Big government had made its first roundup of about 3,000 people. The issue of free speech came about in *Schenck v. US* in 1919.

The Schenck restrictions came about in response to the Socialist Party's printed urgings to resist the American military draft during World War I. Although people have the right to speak against the draft, inciting others to resist violated the Espionage Act passed by Congress to support the war effort. Justice Oliver Holmes, Jr. gave us the phrase "clear and present danger" when providing a test on speech. The idea of free speech without restrictions slipped when compared to the good of the whole: "You can't yell fire in a crowded theater."[46] Why? Because the resulting panic and desire to escape puts everyone in danger. The 1925 *Gitlow v. New York* had an interesting outcome: the majority rejected the "clear and present danger" standard for the "bad (dangerous) tendency" test, which in effect, brought more restrictions on speech.[47] However, by ruling the 14th Amendment due process provision applied freedom of the press standards equally to state and federal governments, the ruling opened the door for more scrutiny of state legislative attempts to control the press. This expansion came into play in the 1937 *Near v. Minnesota* decision, which removed prior restraint from the press.

---

[46] The actual language in the decision read, "falsely shouting fire in a theater and causing a panic" but the saying has been modified over time and through popular usage.
[47] Not surprisingly, Justice Oliver Wendell Holmes, Jr., joined by Louis Brandeis, dissented in favor of the "clear and present danger" standard.

Prior restraint resulting from a Minnesota statute resulted in Jay Near, a journalist for *The Saturday Press,* being subjected to prohibition from publishing further damaging articles against county attorney, former police officer, and future state governor Floyd Olson. The Supreme Court lifted the restriction with Chief Justice Charles Evan Hughes citing the 14th Amendment as applying freedom of the press to state legislative action. As a result, the Near case is considered fundamental to 1st Amendment rights today.

## IT ALL CAME CRASHING DOWN

*The Great Crash of 1929 began a massive economic collapse, and the subsequent Great Depression crippled and reshaped modern America. With Franklin Roosevelt's response through the New Deal, the average American would accept and expect the federal government to be a part of their daily lives, a very definite break from the past. The Progressive growth of government expanded to unprecedented magnitude. Washington, DC, became the home of big government.*

Be careful what you ask for; in the wrong place at the wrong time; whatever can go wrong, will go wrong: Any negative adage you would like to use applies to Herbert Hoover. Elected at the height of the Roaring Twenties, as consumer products made life easier, as America grew richer, the new president most certainly could not have been prepared for the economic meltdown awaiting the nation.

Hoover came to office with great optimism, stating such in his inaugural address. In September, the stock market began to decline. The sell-off continued from September 4 until October 24, forever known as Black Thursday. Then, October 29 brought Black Tuesday, as the Roaring Twenties ended with a crash, literally and figuratively. As fast as all this seems, the crash began to form many years before.

In the mid-1920s, the first cracks began to appear: the land bubble in Florida burst. Agriculture suffered from low returns, and debt service to inflated purchases became increasingly difficult to service. However, the rest of the economy seemed to move right along until late 1929. The crash of stocks in October 1929 provides the focal

Insidious Changes

event of a US economic tailspin. The downturn became the Great Depression that forever changed the face of America.

The Great Bull Market of the Twenties peaked on September 3, 1929. After that, everything went downhill. For three months, the stock market had appeared to be unstoppable, gaining 110 points in that period (to a high of 452). The initial downturn seemed like a natural correction, not the scenario for the October crash. The losses of October 29 took out one-third of the value of the market. Soon the sale of good stocks to cover the losses on bad stocks exacerbated the decline. Those who hoped to buy bargains found out they soon lost value on their new shares. By 1932, only one-tenth of the 1929 stock value would be retained. By 1933, industrial production, as well as personal income, fell to half of their 1929 values. The three million unemployed of 1929 became 15 million in 1933. There seemed to be no bottom to the economic plunge.

Hoover struggled with the downturn that grew ever worse in the early 1930s. At the depth of the Great Depression, one-quarter of Americans were unemployed. Soup lines were standard in large cities. Penniless and homeless, many "hobos" roamed the countryside looking for work and food. There seemed little hope in the early Thirties.

To make matters worse, in 1930 Congress passed, and Hoover signed, the Hawley-Smoot
Tariff, greatly increasing duties on imports in an attempt to protect American industries. Unfortunately, the only thing the tariff accomplished would be a signal to the rest of the world that they were on their own. Twenty-five countries retaliated with higher tariffs on their imports (items from America included). Sales slowed more as the sky kept falling.

Banks folded at a record pace: 1300 for the year of 1930. Nothing seemed to help the crisis. In 1931, Hoover asked the international community for a moratorium on debts owed to each other. Although met with a favorable response, the action soon faded to fears for the future. Hoover could not conceive of payments directly to individuals, but material relief from the federal government did reach state and local entities. Later in 1931, Hoover gave in to the Reconstruction Finance Corporation (RFC) to aid in the bailout of large companies. However, the crisis continued, and Hoover, along with other Republicans, would be turned out of elected offices in

Insidious Changes

droves.  Franklin D. Roosevelt, governor of New York, would become the 32$^{nd}$ US president promising to implement a "New Deal."

# VI: INSTITUTIONAL TRANSFORMATION

## FIGHTING THE GREAT DEPRESSION WITH THE NEW DEAL

*The New Deal significantly advanced the power and scope of the federal government, an accelerated application of Progressive ideals. Franklin Roosevelt began a period of federal government experimentation and expansion after taking office in 1933. A plethora of alphabet agencies (AAA, CCC, NLRB, etc.) kicked off his New Deal. The hallmark of these programs became the direct transfer of monetary wealth to individual citizens. In the end, the average American would accept and expect the federal government to be a part of their daily economic lives.*

Moving forward just a few years in our time travel, we find the once optimistic country on its knees, struggling to move forward with economic growth. There is a real fear of people starving to death. Even those with money worry about when economic opportunity might reappear, not only for those struggling with unemployment but for every American. A brighter future, something that always seemed possible in America, now takes a back seat to sheer survival. Therefore, a strong president seems a necessity for national survival, and as a result, the next Roosevelt expands presidential power with little opposition from the public or Congress.

Winning the election of 1932, President Franklin Roosevelt (FDR) promised Americans they had only fear to fear! When he took office in 1933, he launched the New Deal that spurred the federal government on an unprecedented growth trend that remains intact today. Government programs such as the Agricultural Adjustment Act (AAA), the Civilian Conservation Corps (CCC), Works Progress Administration (WPA), and many others placed federal dollars directly into local economies, often into the pockets of citizens. The Hundred Days, as the beginning of FDR's administration is known, became a flurry of governmental activity. Take note of these events occurring from March through June in 1933:

- A banking holiday to end bank runs and Congress passed the Emergency Banking Relief Act to reopen them with increased governmental regulation.
- Federal salaries were cut by a minimum of 15 percent (the Economy Act).
- The Reforestation Relief Act established the Civilian Conservation Corps (CCC).
- Congress passed the Agricultural Adjustment Act (AAA) to restore agricultural commodity prices.
- The establishment of the Tennessee Valley Authority started a massive government project to produce electricity.
- The Federal Securities Act added governmental regulations to stock trading.
- The Home Owners Refinancing Act provided refinancing for home mortgages.
- The Farm Credit Act provided low-interest loans for farmers.
- The Glass-Steagall Banking Act restricted bank speculation and ensured deposits up to $5,000.
- The National Industrial Recovery Act established the National Recovery Administration (NRA) to participate in such actions as maximum working hours and providing a minimum wage.
- Establishment of the Public Works Administration (PWA).

The British economist John Maynard Keynes (1883-1946, pronounced like "brains" he once told an inquisitor) asserted government intervention would heal the effects of "market failure." Keynes changed the field of economics during the Great Depression. He emphasized employment and the demand side of the economy. President Franklin D. Roosevelt initiated many of Keynes policies during the Depression and they have been with us since that historic time.

Keynes had no problem going against the grain of orthodoxy. He used his literary flare to make his points and usually disarmed his opponents or made them seem silly. However, the biggest key to his success proved to be his willingness to take action while others preached patience.

Keynes asserted that markets might fall into such a deep trough that recovery is a very long-run problem, so long that individuals might lose all they ever had without the prospect of recovering their

Insidious Changes

wealth. As Keynes quipped, "The market can stay irrational longer than you can stay solvent." Keynes' famous line, "In the long-run we're all dead" made his point. He believed that markets worked, just not always as fast as needed. If a person is 40 years old, the economy goes into a depression, and 20 years later the economy recovers, the person has lost the best earning years of his/her life. In other words, for people the short-run is the key. As a result, he proposed several governmental remedies to shorten the recovery.

To "prime" the economy and sped recovery, Keynes suggested deficit spending by the government. This would stimulate demand, requiring supply, which, of course, required labor to produce. This went against the time-honored approach of balanced budgets favored at the time. However, at least theoretically, when the economy recovered, the government could use a revenue surplus to retire the debt. Of course, this is the part that usually fails to occur; politicians seem to be addicted to spending.

Keynes flew in the face of most orthodoxy of his time: the gold standard is too restrictive and fiat money (issued by the government without gold backing) is preferable for a growing economy, savings hurts an economy whereas spending stimulates economic activity, protectionism has a purpose if the national economy needs help, and inflation could achieve full employment. All of these ran counter to many neoclassic theories, the dominant economic philosophy of the time.

Priming the consumer pump with cash to citizens, Keynes argued, would allow the economy to recover from its idle position, and then, and only then, could it grow from its own accord (sometimes when an engine is ran dry of fuel, priming is required to restart it). First and foremost, under-consumption must be cured! However, despite record Washington spending, the American economy struggled throughout the Thirties, and the Dust Bowl of the Great Plains only added to the misery. Despite the setback, the new orthodoxy of Keynes did not lose its luster.[48]

---

[48] Milton Friedman, economic historian and founder of the Monetarist or Chicago School of economics, argued that the Great Depression did not occur because of market failure, but rather because of government action. Friedman proposed that the newly formed Federal Reserve Board took the wrong approach as the financial institutions struggled. As the nation starved for cash, the Feds restricted the money supply in the early 1930s. The economy contracted even more. The bottom did not

Insidious Changes

Senator Huey Long of Louisiana presented a challenge to FDR's New Deal. Long's "Share-our-wealth" campaign launched in 1934 enlisted about seven million people in 1935. "The Kingfish," as he became known, reached a vast audience through radio. He proposed that government should confiscate incomes over $1 million and estates over $3 million. He then promised $2,500 annually to each family, old-age pensions, as well as other government benefits. He seemed destined to run against FDR in 1936, but an assassin's bullet (the son-in-law of a judge he had moved out of office while governor) ended his life and his redistribution campaign in 1935.

With the Economy Act of 1933, FDR ran two budgets: one to be in balance, his regular budget, and the other to be in deficit for a "short" period of time, the emergency budget. Executive Order 6102 outlawed the private holding of gold in 1933, rationalized as a way to prevent hoarding.[49] The following year, the Gold Reserve Act solidified the new rule of no gold ownership for Americans. Citizens had to surrender their gold possessions to the Treasury, which placed the stock in Fort Knox, the gold fortress of the nation (gold ownership and activity remained at least partially prohibited until 1977), and the Treasury ended payouts in gold. The act also devalued the dollar against gold from $20.67 an ounce to $35.

During this period, FDR launched the second phase of his many reforms that changed the nature of federalism focused on more governmental control, and of course, expansion of the federal government. The year 1935 brought:

- Social Security
- Works Progress Administration
- National Youth Administration (financial aid and employment for students)

---

occur until 1933, four years after the Wall Street Crash of 1929. On the other hand, Friedman pointed out, the Panic of 1907, before the advent of the Fed, lasted a year. Was the Great Depression market failure or failure of government? Friedman's conclusion supported the latter interpretation.

[49] Congress had not repealed a World War I law allowing the president to take such action under circumstances of national emergency. With EO 6102, FDR declared the hoarding of gold a national emergency.

- National Labor Relations Board (the Wagner Act legalized collective bargaining, minimum wage established, and 40-hour workweek became law)
- Public regulation of utilities
- Farm Security Administration (aid to farmers)
- Inheritance tax

Today, you can drive across the country and find and an office for the Department of Agriculture in the majority of counties: Social Security facilities cover about a third. As noted above, before the Great Depression the local Post Office would be the only federal presence in most communities. Now, the Feds were everywhere just like state government agencies, right where the average citizen could readily access its programs. This is often referred to in textbooks as marble cake federalism where the two governmental entities, state and federal, live side-by-side. Although states retained most of their police powers, economic and financial duties were solidly under federal purview.

The umbrella of business, agriculture, and labor under the Democrat Party, labeled the New Deal Coalition, seemed to suit the American electorate well at the time as the 1936 presidential election proved to be a landslide victory for FDR. The shift of women and black voters to the Democrat ticket gave him an electoral advantage of 524-7. The wide margin of victory did not end the economic struggle, however.

The economy continued to sputter along, suffering another downturn in 1937 (known as the Roosevelt Recession). Free markets seemed crippled to the educated as well as the uneducated. However, war solved all American economic woes: war on a scale never before witnessed by humanity resulted in a furry of industrial production. Every able-bodied person found employment in the early 1940s, but the Depression Generation never forgot that prosperity could be fleeting, and always feared that hard times could be just around the corner.

### OTHER SIGNIFICANT CONSTITUTIONAL EVENTS OF THE NEW DEAL ERA

*Two significant amendments were added during FDR's first few*

Insidious Changes

*years. The 20ᵗʰ Amendment moved the presidential inauguration date
from March 4 to January 20. Additionally, the grand experiment of
Prohibition ended with the 21ˢᵗ Amendment. Also, an initially
reluctant Supreme Court got on board with the New Deal after threats
of court-packing by FDR: it became known as the "Switch in Time
that Saved Nine." Finally, Congress gave new bilateral negotiation
powers to the president to relax international trade tensions.*

Several significant events occurred during FDR's presidency,
including two amendments. The 20ᵗʰ Amendment moved the date of
convening Congress to January 3 and the presidential oath to January
20. This change came about from the delay of FDR's first election
win in early November 1932 to his taking office on March 4, 1933.
During this period, the financial future of the country hung in the
balance as the lame-duck Hoover struggled and could not institute
constructive change. The president-elect may or may not have been
able to offer help, but no significant crisis legislation emerged during
the period. When FDR took office, 80 percent of the country's banks
were closed: FDR closed the remainder on a four day holiday as the
first legislation of the New Deal passed through Congress. Partly on
the argument to capture new tax revenue, the ratification of the 21ˢᵗ
Amendment ended Prohibition. These amendments came easily, but
the Supreme Court proved to be a substantial challenge to the New
Deal agenda.

Although the Supreme Court had already crept into areas of
traditional state authority, the New Deal seemed to have hesitation.
On Black Monday (May 27) in 1935, the Court led by Charles Evan
Hughes gave three defeats to New Deal programs, the most important
being the Schechter decision which undid Congressional regulations,
passed under the commerce clause, on the poultry industry. The
Court seemed to have the upper hand. However, after an
overwhelming electoral victory in 1936, FDR felt confident in taking
on his robed challengers. Roosevelt's court-packing plan sought to
include additional justices for every member over 70 (the
conservative members). The justification: older justices needed
assistance with the heavy workload. For the first time, FDR found
vehement resistance.

Southern Democrats, conservative at heart, held no love for the
proposal. Republicans, of course, were opposed. The insult to the

Insidious Changes

elderly struck deep. Roosevelt expended a great deal of goodwill and found few political allies. However, for whatever reason, Justice Owen Robert changed his voting stance shortly after the unveiling of the court-packing plan. The Court began to decide in favor of the New Deal, and in substance, FDR won the battle and withdrew his proposal from Congress. "The switch in time that saved nine," became a famous quote, and opened the door for new constitutional powers for the federal government.

As much as FDR struggled with the Court to claim power, Congress seemed to hand it over quite willingly. Crafted from the work of the Brownlee Committee, the Reorganization Act of 1939 solidified power in the executive branch and instituted the Executive Office of the President.[50] Executive order authority would be strengthened to prepare the country in times of increasing global conflict. Executive orders would include 9066 and infamous relocation of Japanese-Americans (upheld by the Court in the Korematsu case, 1944), and 8773 when the president ordered the Secretary of War to take control of National American Aviation to continue the production of "democracy's arsenal."

To ease economic and international tension, Congress gave the president a new path to trade deals, giving the executive broad bilateral (county-to-country) negotiating authority. With the Hawley-Smoot Act compounding the global depression rather than relieving the American economic woes, Congress granted the FDR administration an opportunity to fast track a reverse course by negotiating bilateral tariff reductions with other nations. Equipped with this tool, the FDR administration slowly moved to increased international engagement, opening the door for the US to pursue a course of actively promoting free trade after World War II and continuous efforts to remove protective tariffs.[51]

---

[50] The Executive Office of the President consists of four departments: the White House Staff which includes the Office of Management and Budget, the Vice President, executive departments (15 cabinet departments), and executive independent agencies such as NASA, FCC, etc.

[51] Alexander Hamilton proposed tariff protection for America's developing economy. Hamilton's *Report on Manufactures* proposed: 1) protection of emerging American industries (high tariffs), 2) building physical infrastructure (never fully funded in Antebellum US), and 3) building fiscal infrastructure (assumption plan had vehement opposition but the Dinner Table Compromise brought resolution

Insidious Changes

# WAR AND THE ECONOMY

*Once again, total war redefined the federal government's role in the economy. Trying to make certain that resources went to necessary production, and attempting to keep the economy from overheating with inflation, the Feds found themselves quite busy. The efforts worked successfully to end the war, but left policymakers with a taste for centralized economic control: the temptation would persist for several years after the war.*

War grew closer in the late 1930s. The 1937 Neutrality Act banned the sale of war material to belligerent nations. As the US, Britain, and France did little to address Hitler, the bolder he became. Inch by inch, he grabbed territory around Germany, *Lebensraum* or living space for the Germans. Hitler provided a preview of mechanized warfare in support of his ally Francisco Franco in the Spanish Civil War, but still the US and Western Europe did little to truly prepare for this existential threat. Finally, the invasion of Poland on September 1, 1939 set off World War II. Roosevelt reaffirmed American neutrality on September 5, but policy changes short of entering the war came quickly. By the end of the year, the US had a cash and carry policy for warring nations to purchase war material:

---

[between Hamilton and Madison at Jefferson's invite]) allowed assumption of state debt (with $1.5 million going to Virginia) and placed the US capitol on the Potomac River.

Hamilton proposed a broad interpretation of elastic clause to increase Congressional power over the American economy. His *First Report on Public Credit* resulted in the Dinner Table Compromise, while his *Second Report on Public Credit* produced the First Bank of the United States (in 1791, also the year of a substantial excise tax on liquor). Bonds were issued by the bank (paper securities) to achieve Hamilton's belief that the Bank would solidify the national economy (as opposed to loyalties to state economies and possible succession).

Tariff protection, named the American System by Henry Clay in 1824, became part of the platform of the Whig Party and John Q. Adams (it was also known as National System and Protective System). High tariffs found opposition in the South because as primary producers they favored lower tariffs on imports. Lincoln, influenced by Henry C. Carey's *Harmony of Interests*, ushered in high tariffs that dominated after 1861. The high tariffs remained into the 1930's, reaching a crescendo with the Hawley-Smoot Act.

Insidious Changes

this meant the Allies, mostly Britain and France. A peacetime draft began in 1940 and defense spending increased. To appease public sentiment and the America First movement led by flight pioneer Charles Lindberg, FDR promised to keep American boys out of foreign wars and easily won an unprecedented third term in November.

When Britain could no longer pay for their war goods in 1941, FDR devised the Lend-Lease program to keep the British war effort afloat (literally, this kept the supply flotillas to the island nation in operation). When Hitler invaded the Soviet Union, American Lend-Lease found its way to the Muscovites. In the dark days of August 1941, Churchill met with FDR in the North Atlantic, and American policy began to turn to shaping the goals of fighting. With a superior bargaining position, FDR coerced Churchill into accepting the Atlantic Charter. This policy promised an end to colonialism and increased the cooperation among nations (what would become the United Nations). As the respective leaders returned home, the US entry into the largest armed conflict in history loomed on the horizon.

Although Churchill must have had heartburn after previously making the comment that he had not become prime minister to preside over the collapse of the empire, but on the other hand he could take great comfort in having American support. The American production capacity would be critical to an Allied victory. Lend-lease went only so far, and new war machines would be in constant demand. A few months later, any hesitation on the part of US would be eliminated by the Japanese attack on US forces in Hawaii on December 7, 1941.

The Japanese attack on Pearl Harbor brought the US full into World War II. If there remained any doubt, Hitler eliminated this with the German declaration of war on the US just a few days later. The tremendous industrial productive capacity in the US went into full swing. Much like World War I, the federal government reinstalled the war production boards, and the control of wages and prices became standard fare in an effort to control inflation. Anyone not directly involved in combat or a supporting role easily found a job in the massive industrial complex that went into high gear in an effort to produce everything the average GI needed to be successful: and they would prove to be very successful. By late summer 1945, all Axis nations had surrendered and American policymakers had a globe

Insidious Changes

to rebuild, well, at least that part of the globe not occupied by Soviet troops. As the postwar era unfolded, the hope for peace seemed to hinge more on economic success as opposed to bullets.

Insidious Changes

# VII: SOLIDIFYING THE TRANSFORMATION

## FORESHADOWING IN THE FOUR FREEDOMS SPEECH

*During the State of the Union Address on January 6, 1941, 11 months before Pearl Harbor and the US entry into World War II, FDR revealed the mentality of the Progressive and a plan for the future. Mostly summarized in the Freedom from Want, the Progressives outlined a plan of government involvement to secure economic security for all.*

When our time travel drops us into the late summer and early fall months of 1945, we find a nation in celebration. The "boys" are returning from the war, and minds are on reunions. However, the euphoria soon begins to fade to reality. What about a job? What about building a family? What about a place to live? What about personal transportation. Much of this has been addressed by policymakers in Washington who hoped to "readjust" the economy after the dizzying rate of wartime production slowed (the official name of the bill was the Servicemen's Readjustment Act of 1944).

The GI Bill, passed before the fighting ended, provides choices for realigning lives after the sacrifices of war. Start a business, learn a trade, or attend a four-year college, or take some time to find a paying job: all are available for returning soldiers. The government is taking care of people!

After the war, soldiers flooded to study and work, and after serving in units of tight camaraderie during battle, joining civic organizations seemed natural. They had learned the chain of command in the military, and they would do their part while those more suited filled elected positions in Washington. The problem evolved into that many in Washington became convinced that the federal government is the solution. The government will take care of the economy and provide security, just like it coordinated the effort to win the war!

In his 1941 State of the Union Address to Congress, FDR had already delivered his vision of governmental control of the economy when he outlined his four freedoms. These freedoms were:

- Freedom of the press and expression

~ 93 ~

- Freedom of religion
- Freedom from want
- Freedom from fear

Progressivism, modern liberalism, whatever label is applied, the president openly revealed his penchant for government control. Of course, this was nothing new for FDR, who pursued an active state throughout the New Deal. However, he cemented a legacy with the Four Freedoms, a legacy that has influenced American government ever since, and Congress followed his guidance as the war came to a close. The Freedom from Want expressed the liberal economic planks that would be the most used during the postwar era. In 1946, Congress passed the Employment Security Act seeking to establish these two freedoms. Of course, FDR had already implemented Social Security that sought to eliminate want and fear for those who lived long enough to collect (the retirement age was initially set at 65 when life expectancy for males was 56). Also, the affirmation of a healthy life came into this plank and would become a consistent push for national health care.[52]

Modern liberalism formally replaced so-called "negative" rights (read as protection, or restraint, from government power) for theories of "positive" rights (read as governmental activism) articulated by English philosopher T. H. Green during the late 19th Century. The eventual overwhelming victory of the Allies boosted the idea of government coordination to overcome challenges. Also, the popular opinion that big government resolved the Great Depression (rather than war production, which ended high unemployment and low investment) contributed to the growth of big government around the world. It would reach its US peak without challenge during the Great Society, legislated under President Lyndon Johnson, and financed under his successor Richard Nixon.

---

[52] James Bovard revealed FDR's further plans for extension of government power over industrial production in "The 'Four Freedoms' Speech: FDR's Worst Perversion of Freedom," retrieved from https://fee.org/articles/the-four-freedoms-speech-fdr-s-worst-perversion-of-freedom/?gclid=EAIaIQobChMIiey53dPO5gIVDNvACh0tKAJcEAAYAiAAEgL48PD_BwE.

Insidious Changes

# CONSTANT WAR AND GOVERNMENTAL CHANGE

*World War II and the Cold War put the US in the unfamiliar roles of playing global military police while being a primary force in shaping global politics.*

Before the war ended, the US began to create international institutions that would define the postwar world. The International Monetary Fund, the World Bank (originally established to help rebuild Europe after the war), the United Nations, and the General Agreement on Tariffs and Trade (now the World Trade Organization designed to reduce tariffs and facilitate trade between and among nations) were all set in motion by the Allied victory. The reluctant Americans began to exert world leadership during World War II and understand the need to continue with that leadership after the conclusion of the fighting. American leaders envisioned a world of liberal politics and economics: democracies, free trade, and peace. That was the hope of American policymakers with the conclusion of World War II. Countries that have a stake in each other's success would be "good neighbors" so to speak. However, not everything turned out the way American policymakers hoped.

The war solved many long-standing tensions in Europe but also created new tensions. The Allies mobilized and cooperated at an unprecedented level throughout the war, but quickly solidified into opposing camps with the defeat of Germany and Japan. A new kind of war developed. The US and the Soviet Union found themselves locked in a competition for territory and influence not only in Europe but also around the globe. Injected into this clash of titans brought Harry Truman from Missouri to the forefront.

In Franklin Roosevelt's last run as president, Democrat opponents of Vice President Henry A. Wallace (too liberal for some Democrats of the time) won the day convincing the president to choose a new running mate. The new vice-presidential candidate became Harry S. Truman, a Missouri senator who reluctantly accepted the position. With little doubt of the outcome and Roosevelt in poor health, the clock ticked for Truman to become the 33rd president, which occurred with the death of Roosevelt on April 12, 1945.

As the war wound down, FDR believed he could continue to work with Stalin cooperatively. However, Truman, soon to be FDR's

Insidious Changes

successor, became increasingly suspicious of the Soviet leader. As a result of the growing tension, Truman's administration set the stage for the next 45 years of American foreign policy, the era known as the Cold War. The Cold War brought about a continual state of military readiness, something alien to the American historical experience. Truman would oversee this initial expansion after the war, but first, he had to win the war.

By the time Truman took the oath to become president, Europe had been mostly decided, but Asia offered more of a challenge. Bloody fighting on the Pacific islands under Japanese occupation resulted in high casualties. Finally, the prospect of invading the Japanese main island, with possibly one million Allied casualties, turned Truman to the newest weapon in the American arsenal (when Truman became president, he knew nothing of the Manhattan Project charged with building the atomic bomb). The Enola Gay dropped the first atomic bomb on Hiroshima, August 6, 1945. A follow up on August 9 at Nagasaki finally brought the Japanese surrender on August 14. The largest human conflagration in history ended with a show of force unimagined just a few years earlier.

When the guns fell silent, the politics took over, and the division of Europe between the US and the Soviet Union became a solidified reality. Threats of communist insurgencies in Greece and Turkey prompted the Truman administration to establish the policies that remained an American bulwark throughout the Cold War. Containment sought to stop the Soviet advance in Europe and other areas of the globe. The Truman Doctrine assisted forces resisting communist revolutionaries, but this was only one element of the Truman policy.

The Marshall Plan provided financial assistance to allies, a successful program that revitalized Western Europe by the early 1950s. In the early years of the Cold War, George F. Kennan, a diplomat in Moscow, wrote the Long Telegram explaining the paranoia of Stalin and the Russians in general. Clark Clifford and George Elsey elaborated on US-USSR relations in a private report to Truman (the Clifford-Elsey Report). An article in the journal *Foreign Affairs*, entitled "The Sources of Soviet Conduct" (signed by Kennan as "X" and is therefore known as the "X" Article) outlined what became the policy of containment. Winston Churchill (in the British minority party at the time, and not the prime minister) visited

Westminster College in Fulton, Missouri, and used the phrase "Iron Curtain," referring to the partition of Europe. He urged an alliance between the US and Britain. The Marshall Plan (because Truman had so much controversy with the Republican Congress, he decided to short title the European Recovery Program after his war hero Secretary of State George Marshall) sought to rebuild Western Europe and stop communist "creep." Dean Acheson, later Secretary of State, also proved to be essential in developing the North Atlantic Treaty Organization (NATO) the defense pact between the US and its European allies (1949). The Soviets would counter with their defensive arrangement across Eastern Europe, known as the Warsaw Pact.

The struggle in Germany, a microcosm of Europe, led to the Berlin Airlift of 1948-9. The Soviets, dissatisfied with American policy, cut off ground access to Berlin (situated deep in the Soviet-occupied zone, but divided itself into Western and Soviet sections). The Allies agreed to keep West Berlin free and began airlifting supplies to the city. An incredible mass of foodstuffs and fuel were transported, ultimately resulting in the Soviets dropping the blockade. Stalin lost the initial round in Germany, and containment became a permanent plank in American foreign policy.

Initially, the US sent about $13 billion to Western European countries. The Soviets rejected the offer for themselves their and Eastern European allies, eventually developing their Molotov Plan and establishing the Council for Mutual Economic Assistance, Comecon. The Marshall Plan established the Organization for European Economic Cooperation and began the path to the European Union of today. Comecon, relying heavily on barter, is no longer in existence. As Eastern Europe struggled to recover, Western Europe entered a period of unprecedented growth.

Recovery, however, still left the German question. The Joint Chiefs of Staff directive 1067 (JCS 1067) included the Morgenthau Plan that sought to restrain the growth of German industry, making sure the Huns could never again produce the weapons of war on a scale to threaten Europe. However, Truman commissioned a study under the direction of Herbert Hoover (the former president) that proposed a viable Europe needed an economically healthy Germany and this required industry: this became JCS 1079 and extended aid to rebuild Germany.

Insidious Changes

In 1947, Truman also reorganized the military with the Department of Defense (establishing the Air Force as a separate branch). He also formed the Central Intelligence Agency with the National Security Act of the same year. He certainly provided focus at the outset of the Cold War, and the Republican Congress followed his foreign policy lead. However, another international test brought tension between the two branches.

On June 25, 1950, the Soviet ally of North Korea (the peninsula had been divided at the end of World War II between the US and the USSR) attacked across the 38th parallel. The communist forces pushed American troops to a perimeter around Pusan in the south. Truman rallied the UN to denounce the action and send troops. General Douglas MacArthur landed an amphibious force north in Inchon Bay and surrounded the northern troops. They retreated, and MacArthur drove them back toward China. The Chinese then entered the war, and what seemed like a decisive victory turned into continuous, bitter fighting. MacArthur called several times for strikes against China. A public feud ensued, ultimately ending when Truman relieved MacArthur of his command. MacArthur returned home to a hero's welcome and the intention of running for president against his former boss. However, this plan failed to pan out.

Growing public dissatisfaction with the progress of the Korean Conflict, coupled with the fall of China to the communist followers of Mao Zedong in 1949, precluded Truman from running in 1952. Certainly, Truman's removal of the popular MacArthur from Korea did not boost the president's approval rating in the polls. However, the Republicans went with another war hero over MacArthur: Dwight Eisenhower, former Supreme Allied Commander of World War II. Ike campaigned to end the Asian war, and after winning the presidency did sign a ceasefire with North Korea in 1953 (there is no formal treaty yet today, just a ceasefire).[53]

## TRUMAN, A CONSERVATIVE DEMOCRAT?

*An analysis of the record returns a no. Although often referred to as*

---

[53] Presidential service would be restricted by the 22nd Amendment ratified by the states in 1951. The amendment restricts presidents to two terms (or ten years), a reaction to FDR's four electoral wins.

*such, Truman had a domestic agenda that did not satisfy the true Conservative Democrats of the South. In fact, they would oppose his run for president in 1948, organizing as the Dixiecrats. He exercised in a strong executive position that expanded federal presence in the economy, laid out an aggressive social agenda (modeled on the Four Freedoms) that has served as a Democrat policy blueprint ever since, desegregated the military, and saw another constitutional amendment adopted.*

While facing the Soviets abroad, Truman had an equally tough opponent at home with the Republicans in Congress. As a result, his domestic agenda did not fare so well. Truman's Fair Deal platform, with many social programs, did not go far in Congress. In fact, he did not propose it until after the election of 1948. On January 5, 1949, Truman proposed 21 points and stated that Americans should expect a "fair deal" from their government. The points included these features:

- National health insurance.
- The expansion of unemployment coverage.
- An increased minimum wage.
- Continuing federal price controls.
- Statutory guarantees of full employment.
- Extending job services and federal aid to ex-GIs.
- Increasing agricultural aid.
- Housing legislation.
- Tax reform.
- Increased aid to small businesses.
- Expansion of public works projects.

Despite passing on the Fair Deal, the Progressive tendency of governmental regulation continued to grow. Shortly after the war, Congress passed the Employment Act of 1946, forming the president's Council of Economic Advisors, the Joint Economic Committee, and requiring the Economic Report of the President due to Congress ten days after the president's submission of the annual budget proposal. Congress furthered its economic activity with the Housing Act of 1949, expanding the Federal Housing Administration (FHA, established by the Housing Act of 1934) and allowing the loaning of money to rural dwellers. The act also provided for urban renewal and public housing projects. Always controversial, Truman

~ 99 ~

faced tough opposition on the civil rights front. Eventually, he desegregated the military by executive order in 1948 and also outlawed discrimination in federal employment (undoing the federal segregation of Woodrow Wilson).

Overseas Truman ran into difficulty within his cabinet in 1948 over the recognition of Israel. As the British withdrew from the Mediterranean area, the Jewish community pushed for a state of their own. Marshall adamantly opposed diplomatic recognition of the new state, but Truman ignored him. Marshall told him how vehemently he disagreed, but Truman lobbied other allies within the UN to recognize Israel. Truman won this fight, and Marshall resigned.

With all this buzzing about Truman, the experts considered him a certain loser in the election of 1948 (the Democrats were severely divided by Dixiecrats formed in the South). However, experts can be wrong, and Truman pulled out the presidency in a tight race against Thomas Dewey.


## TRUMAN'S STRUGGLES WITH THE STEEL INDUSTRY

*Truman believed he had authority, exercised by previous presidents, to ensure war production. A threatened steel production strike loomed, and in Truman's estimation, so did a potential disruption of war production (at the time, steel served as the primary material for airplanes). However, in the end, Truman would be rebuked by the Court, and an outline of the three categories of presidential power would result from the decision.*

With an expanding economy in the early 1950s, wages were often an issue, and so it would be in the steel industry. At the end of 1951, the United Steelworkers of America union threatened to go on strike over a 35 cent hourly increase. The case went to the Wage Stabilization Board, which set the increase to 26 cents, an increase the union accepted. However, steel companies demanded a concurrent rise in steel prices, and as a result, rejected the proposed settlement.

Truman felt confident that the US involvement in Korea would justify his taking control of steel mills, placing them under his Secretary of Commerce. In *Youngstown Sheet and Tube Co. v.*

~ 100 ~

*Sawyer*, the Supreme Court disagreed with the president's interpretation of war emergency powers.

In the decision, the Court rejected the analogy to FDR's seizure of North American Aviation as false. Justice Robert Jackson (who had been involved in the earlier case) laid out three areas of presidential authority in an executive power test that remains intact. Jackson contended that the president has:

- Authority that is specifically listed in the Constitution, and other powers given by Congress. These inherent powers were the most convincing.
- The second area of authority exists as not explicitly provided or denied to the president. Here Congress and the president can live in a sort of truce between them.
- In the final category, the president can only act in accordance with the powers supplied within the Constitution and not encroach upon the powers given to Congress (provides the least amount of executive authority).

A steel industry strike persisted for seven weeks. In the end, the steelworkers took a 21 cent increase, and steel prices raised a little less than half of the original proposal, similar terms that had been proposed earlier by Truman.


## CIVIL RIGHTS ACCOMPLISHMENTS OF THE EARLY POSTWAR ERA

*From Jackie Robinson to the integration of the University of Mississippi, there were several advances in civil rights for Southern blacks after World War II. One of the most significant events came with the 1954 Supreme Court decision of* Brown v. Board of Education *that set the stage for the desegregation of public schools throughout the US. During 1957, Eisenhower enforced the decision in Little Rock, Arkansas, and later Kennedy broke ground in higher education with the desegregation of the University of Mississippi.*

On April 15, 1947, the Brooklyn Dodgers brought desegregation to the national pastime. The Dodgers front office executive Branch Rickey, the man credited for developing the farm system of player development during his tenure in St. Louis, broke more new ground with Jackie Robinson at first base on that fateful April day.[54] The next year President Truman desegregated the US armed forces, and the following year he shepherded the Housing Act of 1949 through Congress bolstering the federal role to provide public housing in urban areas. However, advancements in civil rights began to break loose from a subsequent Supreme Court decision.

In the 1954 decision, *Brown v. Board of Education*, the Court ruled against segregation in public education. This case was a consolidation of several such cases in multiple states as well as the District of Columbia. Heard initially in 1953, the Court did not reach a consensus decision, and Justice Felix Frankfurter recommended a rehearing the following session. Chief Justice Fred Vinson, citing too much judicial activism in implementing desegregation, passed away to be replaced by Earl Warren. Warren presented the argument not so much as unequal facilities, but rather separate facilities violated the equal protection clause of the 14th Amendment. Based on this reasoning, the Court overturned the "separate but equal" principle of *Plessy v. Ferguson* (the Brown case would be the basis of several subsequent cases concerning the desegregation of other public facilities).[55] In a follow-up decision the next year (sometimes referred to as *Brown II*), the Court instructed states to desegregate with "all deliberate speed." However, "all deliberate speed" became a delaying tactic, which was the situation in Arkansas.

Eisenhower enforced the Brown decision in Arkansas. The original decision declared that separate schools were "inherently unequal" and subsequently ordered that segregation should be

---

[54] Professional football had actually integrated a year earlier with Kenny Washington (former University of California-Los Angeles star) and Woody Strode as teammates on the Los Angeles Rams. The upstart All-American Football Conference also had an integrated team, the Cleveland Browns who suited up Bill Willis and Hall of Famer Marion Motley. The Washington Redskins would be the last pro football team to racially integrate in 1962.

[55] An interesting, and controversial, outcome of the decision came from Footnote 11 concerning studies of the psychological effects of segregation on the students. The footnote cited the study of Kenneth B. Clark, a social scientist who studied the effects of desegregation on school children. When presenting white and black dolls to black children, they preferred the white dolls: the implication being that black children had low self-esteem, deeming themselves inferior to white children. The role of the citation in the decision is considered a building block for a more multidisciplinary approach to the law.

~ 102 ~

eliminated "with all deliberate speed." This phrase became the loophole for school administrators and politicians (again, especially in the South) to delay desegregation. Their argument, "We're moving as fast as is practical." Arkansas Governor Orval Faubus used the Arkansas National Guard to restrict the desegregation of Little Rock Central High School. Eventually, President Dwight D. Eisenhower federalized the Guard and forced the desegregation action (Executive Order 10703). The Arkansas governor, with legislative authority, would close Central High and implement the state's new desegregation plan that resulted in token integration. Some other Southern states, notably Virginia, Mississippi, Alabama, South Carolina, and Georgia remained recalcitrant against the new public law.

On another civil rights front, Eisenhower helped guide through Congress the Civil Rights Act of 1957 intended to increase the registration of black voters in the South (only about 20 percent of eligible black voters were actually registered), but heavily watered down after resistance from Southern Democrats. In the end, the law lacked real enforcement measures but did provide for federal referees to oversee elections.

The civil rights movement moved to the streets with defiance from Rosa Parks on a Montgomery bus when she refused to give up her seat to a white passenger. Martin Luther King, Jr. rose to prominence with the ensuing Montgomery Bus Boycott. King's activity began with this boycott that brought him to the national spotlight. He formed the Southern Christian Leadership Committee in 1957 and served as president. He wrote "Letter From a Birmingham Jail" while incarcerated in Alabama, in essence opposing Eisenhower's gradualist approach to desegregation. He led the 1963 March on Washington and saw the passage of the Civil Rights Act in 1964. Although King always advocated non-violence, not everyone agreed with him (the Nation of Islam and the Black Panthers, formed in 1966, both proved to be aggressive).

After the Montgomery Bus Boycott, lunch counter sit-ins spread across the South as did freedom rides on busses to protest the segregation of various public facilities. In 1960, John F. Kennedy won the presidency by a very narrow margin. Although Kennedy had many international events defining his presidency, he made an impact on civil rights. He appointed Thurgood Marshall, plaintiff lawyer in the Brown decision, a federal appellate judge in 1961. Marshall would eventually become the US Solicitor General under Lyndon Johnson, and then a Supreme Court justice. This appointment solidified the Democrat's liberal hold on government as Marshall believed in a "living" constitution to be "adjusted" to current and subsequent social circumstances.[56] Kennedy also advanced the cause of equal opportunity in employment, opposed discrimination in housing, as well as enforced the enrollment of James Meredith at the University of Mississippi in 1962 and confronted Governor George Wallace to admit black students at the University of Alabama. However, despite these efforts, JFK is usually not cited as a driving force of the civil rights movement, a designation usually reserved for his brother, Robert. Bobby proved to be the right-hand man of civil rights for Jack's White House and remained as an author of the civil rights legislation that passed under Lyndon Johnson in 1964 (noted above). So, despite the well-publicized tension between the Kennedy's and LBJ, they made civil rights history together.

## EARL WARREN AND THE ACCELERATION OF JUDICIAL ACTIVISM

*Earl Warren and his associate justices began a reinterpretation of the Bill of Rights, expanding individual rights. Warren took the 14th Amendment and interjected the Court's opinion more and more into what previously had been state authority.*

Earl Warren served as a career politician, beginning with municipal attorney duties and advancing all the way to challenging for the Republican nomination for president. He served as the California Attorney General (1939-43), and the state's governor (1943-53). Warren ran as the vice-presidential nominee in Thomas Dewey's unsuccessful presidential bid against Harry Truman in 1948. In 1952, he ran for the Republican nomination for president but

---

[56] During the 1987 bicentennial celebration of the US Constitution, Marshall made known his belief that it had proven itself to be a flawed document from the beginning requiring several amendments, a civil war, and numerous other struggles to move toward the fulfillment of its promise of equality. He further commented that he considered it a living document that embodied individual freedom.

Insidious Changes

bowed out to Dwight Eisenhower. Eisenhower nominated him for chief justice of the Supreme Court in 1953.

Giving little indication to his judicial inclinations, Warren stamped the Court with a liberal and libertarian tinge that still causes division today. He began almost immediately with the Brown case. The outcome proved to be fair, but the method of arrival to the decision has resulted in judges often becoming super-legislators.

In the 1954 decision, *Brown v. Board of Education*, the Court ruled against segregation in public education. Controversy still surrounds the issue of Court activism in this case: Congress had not passed a desegregation act, the ruling came from an interpretation of the Equal Protection Clause of the 14th Amendment, and the Court, not Congress, ordered desegregation. The follow-up decision instructing states to desegregate with "all deliberate speed" led to President Eisenhower's enforcement of the decision, and the Court continued with several subsequent cases concerning the desegregation of other public facilities. However, this is not the extent of Warren's legacy.

The Warren Court began to increasingly set public policy through court decisions, many of these, but not all, grounded in criminal protections found in the Bill of Rights. These landmark cases and precedents included:

- *Mapp v. Ohio* (1961) applied an exclusionary rule on evidence collected without a search warrant under the 4th Amendment (if evidence came about without a warrant, it would be excluded from the evidence presented at the trial).
- *Engle v. Vitale* (1962) removed state-sponsored bible readings and prayers in public schools.
- *Robinson v. California* (1962) defining cruel and unusual punishment under the 8th Amendment.
- *Gideon v. Wainwright* (1963) extended the right to counsel to non-capital as well as capital punishment cases.
- "One man, one vote" cases from 1962-4 included *Baker v. Carr, Gray v. Sanders*, and *Reynolds v. Sims* all directed at equal representation in legislatures and overriding geographic districts.
- *Miranda v. Arizona* (1966) led to the important ruling that every criminal detainee must be informed and understand their

constitutional rights, including the right to an attorney. This led to the Miranda warning.[57]

- *Loving v. Virginia* (1967) lifted restrictions on interracial marriages.

Little did Eisenhower realize that he had appointed one of the most activist justices in American history: later, Eisenhower lamented about his appointment, describing it as, "The biggest damn-fool mistake I ever made." Despite the buyer's remorse, Warren goes down as one of the most impactful chief justices in the history of the Supreme Court, whether for good or ill. Wherever an observer might fall on the good/bad divided, no one argues the point that Warren changed the trajectory of public policy. However, Warren also played another role in Washington politics.

Warren headed the Warren Commission, appointed by LBJ. After extensive investigation, the Commission found Lee Harvey Oswald acted as the lone gunman in the assassination of JFK. The Commission intended to quell speculation of a conspiracy in the murder of the 35th president, but it failed miserably. As you are most likely well aware, JFK murder conspiracy theories still abound to this day.

Warren tendered his resignation from the Court after the assassination of Robert Kennedy. He cited age but left his departure at the pleasure of LBJ. Rumor has it that he believed Nixon would win the presidency, whom he blamed for his losing 1952 presidential bid, and did not want his old political rival to select his replacement.

## THE GREAT SOCIETY EXPANSION OF GOVERNMENT

*The Great Society serves as the high watermark of modern liberalism*

---

[57] When arrested, for any information to be admissible as trial evidence law enforcement must inform the suspect of their legal rights. This consists of reading a statement informing the defendant that they, 1) right to remain silent, and statements can be used in court. 2) You have the right to an attorney, and the court will appoint one if you cannot afford one. Most of us have heard these on television shows. 3) Some states require that non-citizens are offered the opportunity to contact their lawyer before questioning. 4) Others require that defendants be told they may talk and terminate the interview at any point they wish. In all cases, law enforcement must demonstrate that the defendant understood the rights in their language and/or at their level of education.

*(progressivism) in the US: civil rights expansion, as well as the federal government's physical and authoritative presence, grew immensely. With the liberal hour came an expanded and more intrusive federal government.*

In 1963, the Civil Rights Movement kicked into high gear with the March on Washington (about 200,000 in attendance). Here, Martin Luther King, Jr. gave his famous "I Have a Dream" speech calling for all Americans to be judged on "the content of their character, not the color of their skin." The theme resonated well with the media and civil rights activists, but little happened until after JFK's assassination in Dallas on November 22. This event fueled the fire of reform through an unlikely champion, the new president, and Southern Democrat Lyndon B. Johnson.

Johnson took JFK's civil rights bill, bogged down in the Senate, and used his legislative savvy to push it through. He based it on the commerce clause believing this to be the best survival mechanism through the Supreme Court. He gambled correctly, and the Court upheld the 1964 Civil Rights Act in *Heart of Atlanta Motel v. US* and *Katzenbach v. McClung*. Both proved to have very substantial legal foundations, even to the point of enforcing at a very local level. The Heart of America Hotel decision proved to be much like the Wickard decision in that even very minute and indirect interstate activity would be subject to Congressional power under Article I, Section 8, Clause 3 (commerce clause).[58]

In 1964, President Lyndon Johnson began promoting his social welfare reform program designed to eliminate suffering from poverty, controllable diseases, poor education, and racial injustice. In November, LBJ won a landslide victory over Barry Goldwater and swept in a Democrat-supermajority Congress. With control of the House and 60 votes in the Senate, the Great Society rolled out with no real opposition.

- Economic Opportunity Act spending nearly $1 billion to fight a "war on poverty."

---

[58] John L. Bullion, "Lyndon B. Johnson," in Ken Gromley, ed., *The Presidents and the Constitution*. New York: New York University Press, 2016, 477-9.

Insidious Changes

- Appalachian Regional Development Act, again spending $1 billion in 11 states from Pennsylvania to Alabama to overcome poverty in this mostly rural area.
- The food stamp pilot program became permanent (relaxed qualifying criteria came in 1977).
- Medicare Act provided health care to the elderly through Social Security payments.
- Medicaid, administered in cooperation with states, provided means-tested health insurance.

The Johnson administration also enlarged the size, as well as the spending, of the federal government. New departments included:
- Department of Housing and Urban Development
- Department of Transportation
- The Public Broadcast Act of 1967 laid the foundation of the Corporation for Public Broadcasting, Public Broadcast System, and National Public Radio.

As well as several legislative acts, including:
- The 24th Amendment outlawed poll taxes.
- Civil Rights Act of 1964, which among other things, established the Equal Employment Opportunity Commission. Johnson instituted Affirmative Action by executive order (EO 10925).
- Voting Rights Act of 1965 gave teeth to the 15th Amendment after violence in Selma, Alabama.
- Immigration reform (1965).
- Civil Rights Act of 1968 banned discrimination in housing and provided constitutional rights to Indians on reservations.

Johnson and the liberals had few qualms about stepping on state authority, and they had ample help. In 1965, an unknown lawyer wrote *Unsafe at Any Speed* critiquing the Chevrolet Corvair. Ralph Nader became a consumer advocate and began a push to grow government in ways not included in the Great Society. Automobile regulations came first, but certainly not last.

The Corvair (a combination of the names Corvette and Bel Air) served as the focal point of Nader's critique concerning the lack of safety in the automobile industry as a whole. The Corvair did have some problems with steering, and the back placement of the engine added to the issue; however, the Corvair may not have been less roadworthy than any other car at the time, but it did gather attention.

The point Nader made, focused on safety taking a backseat, so to speak, to style and performance. The 1960s, the V-8 engine, sleek lines, and chrome: safety lost out to the pursuit of image. Nader went to Congress to correct this oversight of priorities and walked away with a fantastic growth rate for the administrative state.

Automobile safety laws led the way in 1966, but these just opened the door. With the founding of the Center for the Study of Responsive Laws, Nader became the point of the spear for air and water quality regulation, more automobile safety as well as occupational safety, food quality, the Freedom of Information Act, nuclear power regulation, as well as other areas of reform. Nader founded or helped found various organizations such as the Center for Auto Safety, the Clean Water Action Project, the Pension Rights Center, and several others. However, the residual of all this became more bureaucracy and more red tape. The Occupational Safety and Health Administration (OSHA), Environmental Protection Agency (EPA), and the Consumer Product Safety Commission (CPSC).

Congress went with the roll: the Wholesome Meat Act of 1967 required states to inspect meat with an "equal" quality of federal inspections. A plethora of federal environmental laws would be passed. The Feds entered education and sent payments directly to schools and included a flurry of community-based education initiatives, including Head Start. Higher education would also be caught in the net with loans and grants for qualifying students. The previously mentioned Medicaid program would be a "cooperative" program, but the obvious question is, who holds the most power? Throughout the Great Society era, the reach of the federal government grew longer through statute and bureaucracy. However, such questions and potential concerns might have been lost in a utopian mindset. Or maybe the mere fact that so much happened in the 1960s that mundane questions about federalism became lost in the whirlwind of change, and unfortunately, violence.[59]

---

[59] There is no one firm definition of the eras of federalism, but certainly federal authority expanded during LBJ's presidency. Some political scientists refer to the New Deal through the Great Society as cooperative federalism, defining it is the three levels of government (federal, state, and local), but the bottom line is that the federal government has the vast majority of the power. Also, the US Constitution recognizes only states, not local units. The term, although widely used, glosses over the uneven distribution of power and the inconsistency with the Constitution.

Insidious Changes

Violence would reign throughout the South during the 1960s, even with federal intervention. Whites resisted blacks, often with the support of local law enforcement. King continued to try and keep the lid on the Black Movement. The National Association for the Advancement of Colored People (NAACP) and the National Urban League supported the non-violence agenda. However, spontaneous riots in urban ghettos and the formation of the openly militant Black Panthers continually pushed the violence button. The violence rose to the point of murder.

Medgar Evers had been killed in Mississippi in1963. Malcolm X suffered an assassin's bullet in 1965 (three assailants from the Nation of Islam were convicted of murder), and urban riots beginning in the Watts area of Los Angeles spread around the country, the most fierce being in Newark, Detroit, as well as Los Angeles. Even King eventually fell to an assassin's bullet in Memphis on April 4, 1968. Urban riots became even more widespread with the death of King, and with his death came the end of the Second Civil Rights Movement (the first occurring after the Civil War).

In the end, the Great Society greatly expanded the size and scope of the federal government: the largest expansion since the New Deal. However, the Great Society never reached its promise. Some have argued that the associated programs only accomplished a dependent underclass that seeks government subsidies and does not enter the ranks of the gainfully employed. This cycle of poverty, it is argued, passes from generation to generation. Perhaps its promise died in battlefields half a globe away in Vietnam, as MLK suggested. Johnson's attempt to eliminate poverty in America as he also cautiously continued the fight against communist expansion defined his administration and legacy. Perhaps too much faith in government, filled with flawed humans, became the demise of LBJ's big government plans, but his aggressive posture dissipated in Southeast Asia. He left office unable to conquer either poverty or North Vietnam.

# VIII: THE CONSTITUTION DURING THE ERA OF SOCIAL UPHEAVAL

## THE COUNTERCULTURE: FROM BEATS TO HIPPIES

*Not everyone bought into the government solving all problems. In fact, some did not buy into the culture-at-large. The counterculture began to appear more and more in the 1950s, laying the groundwork for an explosion in the 1960s, culminating in Woodstock. Although the hippy had been pronounced dead in 1967, the counterculture influences American society today in opposition to traditional America.*

Probably nothing of the Fifties has caused more ripples in our current American society than the seeds of the counterculture. Born from those who did not follow the traditional American "Ozzie and Harriet" plan, the Beats, and others, began to challenge all conventions, and during the 1960s the youth of America became enthralled.

The term "Beats" refers to a particular group of American writers, later referred to as "Beatniks," tagging on to the Soviet satellite launch. These writers were known for their alternative lifestyles that deviated from the accepted 1950s norm: homosexuality, drug experimentation, and spontaneity all challenged the social mores of the era. (The term "Bohemian hedonists" also refers to this group, harkening back to the Romantic poets of the early nineteenth century.) Among the most famous of these writers were Allen Ginsberg, William S. Burroughs, and Jack Kerouac, often referred to as the Big Three.

Ginsberg broke into prominence with his poem, *Howl*, published in 1956. This poem challenged societal conventions depicting Ginsberg's contacts with the mentally ill. He considered these people to be heroes, the best minds of his generation destroyed by the ravages and demands of industrial society. The poem became part of an obscenity trial, but the judge's decision did not ban the book as he deemed it to have some social value. Another obscenity trial ensued

~ 111 ~

Insidious Changes

early in the 1960s with Burroughs: *The Naked Lunch,* a novel (or somewhat novel) of similar sexual and drug use content contained in *Howl.*[60] Again, the judge ruled that the work had some redeeming social value and did not ban the book. Jack Kerouac, rounding out the Big Three, published *On the Road* in 1957.

Kerouac introduced the term "Beat Generation" to refer to a gathering of alternative writers in New York during 1948: here he met with Ginsberg and Burroughs. Kerouac had previously met Ginsberg at Columbia University. A catalyst for the Beats had come a year before in 1947 when they met Neal Cassady. Ginsberg had an affair with him, and Kerouac took a road trip with him. This trip became the subject of Kerouac's book, with Cassady named David Moriarty in the recounting of their cross-country adventure. Cassady became a countercultural icon with his exploits including drugs, many women, many cars, many towns, and a dearth of cash, but living life to its fullest extent and always on the edge.

The story goes that Kerouac wrote this novel in a three-week spurt when he placed continuous scrolls of computer paper in a typewriter and began writing (too bad he didn't have a word processor). This scenario is an exaggeration, as he had at least two drafts of the work before he took Benzedrine in 1951 and completed his book in a flurry of writing. The book would not be published until 1957, giving the impression that it was current at that time, but the events were nearly a decade old by the time it hit the bookshelves.

Gregory Corso, also known as a Beat (he joined the Big Three in 1950), rounded out the most influential of this group. The Beats would blend in with the San Francisco Renaissance and the Black Mountain poets. All explored alternatives to the conventional, including Eastern philosophy, and tended to gravitate to jazz music. Ginsberg haunted cafes in Berkley, California, so it is easy to understand how the "hippie" movement came together in the western state.

These literary elements of rebellion began to seep into mainstream America. "The Wild One," starring Marlon Brando as a tough biker and the ultimate young movie screen icon James Dean as a "Rebel Without a Cause," all spoke to the impressionable Baby Boom

---

[60] Originally titled, and intended to be named *Naked Lunch*, and sometimes referred to by this name, the first publisher made a printing mistake with the article included.

*Insidious Changes*

generation. These youngsters began to listen to the likes of Elvis Presley and other "rock-n-rollers." Born of increasingly well-to-do parents after World War II, the Baby Boomers had the disposable income to spend on these entertainment items, and so, those astute in business produced more and more of the appealing items. After Sam Phillips made Elvis a staple among American teens, black musicians began to be accepted by the largely white audience. The "45," referring to the rotations per minute of the record, became a generational socializing agent. If you didn't know the latest Elvis tune, or Fats Domino, or Chuck Berry, or Little Richard, why you were "square, man" you just weren't "hip" (this is the first type of "rapping" using slang in a melodic tone).

The fast beat of the music, the frenzied dances, as well as the inclination to unrestrained public behavior, attracted the youth, who, as tends to happen with younger generations, sought to break from the constraints of their parents. The spirit of rebellion spread beyond literature, film, and music as the 1960s dawned.

The Students for a Democratic Society formed in 1960, but their roots went back to the turn of the century as a socialist, labor organization. Students met at Ann Arbor, Michigan in early 1960 and adopted the new name. Tom Hayden (one-time husband of Jane Fonda and former member of the California legislature having served in both chambers) wrote the Port Huron Statement (adopted in 1962) criticizing American politics and foreign policy. The statement also championed a campaign against poverty and nonviolent disobedience of unjust laws. The uniform of the SDS became a blue work shirt, blue jeans, and boots. Eventually, the SDS would become involved in the agitation on college campuses against the war in Vietnam.

Student activism also popped up in California. In October 1964, the University of California, Berkley police placed former graduate student Jack Weinberg under arrest after he refused to leave the campus or show his identification. Students collected around the police car and began a sit-in at the administration building that lasted for 32 hours before the campus police dropped charges. The sit-in continued until the administration moved to arrest the students in December: a larger protest then broke out. The university administration backed off.

The goal of the students began with increased political activity on campus, behavior that the administration restricted to the two major

Insidious Changes

parties (faculty had to take a loyalty oath).  As it continued, it gained momentum serving as a launching point for anti-Vietnam protests.  It also had a backlash effect.  Ronald Reagan won his first political office, Governor of California, campaigning to clean up the "mess" in Berkley.  When Reagan took office, he directed the Board of Regents to dismiss the University of California President Clark Kerr.  However, the cast of alternative characters continued to grow as did alternative behavior.

Timothy Leary bounced around several colleges before finally finishing his bachelor's degree while in the Army during WWII.  After the war, Leary entered graduate school and finally received a doctorate in psychology.  He taught at the University of California, Berkley, and lectured at Harvard.  However, a trip south of the border changed his life.

In Mexico, Leary took some hallucinogenic mushrooms that he said "opened" his mind.  He found them enlightening and began to be an advocate of using "mind-expanding" drugs such as the synthetic LSD being developed by the US government.  He became a counterculture icon with his promotion of "mind expansion" drugs and his saying, "Tune in, turn on, and drop out."  This slogan became the mantra of the hippies.

During the Summer of 1967, the Beats became the Hippies as the counterculture descended upon the Haight-Ashbury District of San Francisco.  Open drug use, sexual promiscuity, and various other alternatives to commercial and mainstream America found the way into the district.

The stream of youth began during Spring Break in 1967.  The Monterrey Pop Festival of June brought more people to the area.  Eventually, the area became overly saturated: the public facilities and housing could not accommodate the mass of humanity.  Criminals soon followed and trouble began.

With over 100,000 people crammed into the urban area, the population overload did not begin to decline until autumn arrived.  Some returned to school.  Some moved to communes in the California countryside.  Some did not survive from drug use, murder, or other problems.  The remaining crowd staged a mock funeral to signify the "Death of the Hippie."  As explained on a Public Broadcasting System special, the message was, don't come here, have your revolution at home.  However, the hippie did not die in the fall of

~ 114 ~

Insidious Changes

1967. Instead, the revolutions at home began to ripple through society, sometimes in a very public and shocking manner.

During the Mexico City Olympic Games in 1968, two American sprinters shocked viewers back home. Gold medalist Tommie Smith and bronze winner John Carlos took the stand for the traditional playing of the winner's national anthem. The sprinters had donned black gloves and raised their fists in the Black Power sign. The fists alluded to militant black groups and immediately met with resistance. The International Olympic Committee with their US counterparts sent the runners packing for violating the rule that politics did not enter the Olympic Games.

In July 1969, cops conducted a routine raid on a mob-run nightclub in New York. The bar had many gay patrons who were mourning the passing of their icon: Judy Garland. Incensed, the crowd fought back. Riots built for several nights after the initial raid. "Gay power" became the chant, and endorsement came from no less a leader than Allen Ginsberg. The gay liberation movement evolved from this event, and it became commemorated around the US with various "Gay Pride" parades and festivities.

The Students for a Democratic Society remained a peaceful organization into the late Sixties. Some members became restless and impatient with what they believed to be the slow pace of change in American society. In 1969, a radical faction broke off to go on its own. The Weathermen (also known as the Weather Underground) sought to activate the downtrodden of society, including the Black Panthers. They also sought to bring the war home and planned a series of bombings in the US. This group participated in various acts of violence, incited riots, and conspired to spread their revolution throughout the country. Unlike the path of education, the SDS leadership followed, the Weathermen sought violent action to make the revolution happen, and they were not alone. However, it might have been one long-haired, bearded male who branded the counterculture as dangerous. Perhaps no name from the Sixties brings more shudders than that of Charles Manson.

Born the illegitimate son of a prostitute, Manson drifted into a life of crime (burglary, sodomy, prostitution), eventually moving from his native Ohio to California. There he made his mark. California held young adults, and adolescents, of easy prey. Manson found many of them in Haight-Ashbury during the Summer of Love. Those who ran

Insidious Changes

away from home thought they found a friend in Manson, and he began to form a "family" around himself. What they found was a manipulative, brainwashing criminal with a radical worldview.

Manson believed the white race to be superior, and a race war to be just around the corner. In this state of mind, he found coded messages in the Beatles' "White Album" (a plain white cover with an imprint of "The Beatles" stamped on the cover resulted in this nickname). Once this war got underway, Manson believed the white race would take its rightful place in the world. Unfortunately, he believed, the whites had become soft and had to be prodded into this fight. So, Manson thought he would lend a hand.

Using his followers from his Southern California compound, Manson's Family cruised the Los Angeles area until they found a victim: they began in late July with musician Gary Hinman. Early in August, they found Sharon Tate, an upcoming star ("Valley of the Dolls") and eight months pregnant from director Roman Polanski. The murder was brutal, but Manson himself did not enter the house. An equally brutal murder came the next night with the murder of the businessman Leno LaBianca and his wife. Rosemary had been stabbed 41 times with "Helter Skelter" (a song title from the "White Album") scrawled on the refrigerator door in the victims' blood. When the police tracked the perpetrators to the Manson compound, they found the leader tucked away under a sink cabinet.

The trial became a mockery. Manson carved a swastika into his forehead. Three girls on trial for murder shaved their heads and sang during the trial. Finally, a conviction came, and Manson received the death sentence. However, the California Supreme Court reduced the gallows poll to life sentences. Manson remained in prison until his eighties when he died. He remains as a symbol, rightly or wrongly, as a testament to the counterculture gone wrong stealing youth and their innocence, leaving them hollow and treacherous. However, to be fair, not all of the counterculture in the late Sixties proved to be violent.

In August 1969, the counterculture descended upon a dairy in upstate New York. The apex of the hippie generation came to rural America for "Three Days of Peace and Music." Max Yasgur's farm, located southwest of the village of Woodstock, hosted the event that promised about 200,000 attendees. Double that number showed up. The locals were suspicious that so many young people might cause problems, but the crowd remained at the farm and minded the music and the ancillary activities. Two deaths occurred: one a heroin overdose and the other from an accident when a tractor moving across a field met an occupied sleeping bag. The blaring music of Janis Joplin, Jimi Hendrix (who played the Star-Spangled Banner on his electric guitar with his teeth), The Who, Santana, Jefferson Airplane, and others captured what is often considered the apex of the counterculture. However, the open and rampant nudity, drug use, and sexual activity shocked traditional America back home. This visual came on the heels of another very telling episode of the clash between opposing visions of life in the US.

## THE END OF THE NEW DEAL COALITION

*On the rise throughout the 1960s, the counterculture peaked in its opposition to the old order during the 1968 Democrat National Convention held in Chicago. The tattered party that left the Windy City entered the fall election cycle worse for the wear and began to lose former supporters beginning with the Solid South.[61] The first cracks of belief in government providing progress and prosperity began to appear in general society.*

The American political scene had been mostly stable since the New Deal. Democrats almost always controlled Congress, and except for Eisenhower, they also controlled the presidency. Northern Democrats passed their social programs, and the Southern Democrats were generally left alone. Republicans often held a strong voice in foreign affairs with their strong opposition to communism. The political world had a comfort zone of a sort, but this arrangement ended in 1968.

The war in Vietnam had stirred a great deal of opposition among American youth throughout the decade. While campaigning for president in 1964, Johnson had commented that "American boys should not be in Asia doing what Asian boys ought to be doing for

---

[61] In reaction to the forced reforms of Reconstruction from the Republicans, Southerners typically voted solidly for Democrats, a pattern that persisted for about a century. However, the turmoil of the 1960s strained this tradition and voting for Republicans became acceptable.

themselves." This statement proved to be campaign rhetoric, and after the election, the escalation in Vietnam ratcheted upward. As the number of troops in Southeast Asia grew, so did the number of demonstrators on college campuses, a group that became increasingly confrontational. The Civil Rights Movement became increasingly violent, and more resistance to traditional American values began to emerge. The counterculture had reached maturity and resilience. To this day, a divided America exists between Traditional America (that we associate with Norman Rockwell) and the counterculture. The two cultures have resulted in cultural tension, a generation gap, and a broken political system.

In early 1968, North Vietnamese troops poured into the south on the Vietnamese New Year. The Tet Offensive caught Americans and South Vietnamese off guard, and they took some time to organize a resistance. American news cameras were rolling all the time and portrayed the event as an American defeat, and the public went with the news services. Ironically, the North ultimately suffered a huge defeat losing about two-thirds of its military capability. The problem, the Americans and the South Vietnamese never followed up on this infliction of military damage. However, the political damage fell on the US, and the consequences proved to be enormous.

In the New Hampshire primary, LBJ lost to anti-war candidate Hubert Humphrey. Johnson announced he would not seek reelection (because of opposition to the fighting in Vietnam). The wheels began to come off, and that summer, the Democrat National Convention (DNC) erupted in violence, and the party fell into disarray.

In late August 1968, the Counterculture clashed with more Traditional America in Chicago. The DNC became the scene of violent encounters that showed the TV viewers at home just how far political stress had driven opponents.

Abbie Hoffman and Jerry Rubin formed the Yippies, the Youth International Party, to bring their politics to the Democrat National Convention. They also brought their candidate, Pigasus (a pig!), to make a pitch to head the top of the presidential ticket.

Chicago Mayor Richard Daley (a.k.a. the Kingmaker) was determined to keep the youthful protestors under control. The demonstrators moved in on the convention site and played to the cameras from August 25-28. Daley had 12,000 police and reinforced them with National Guard troops who were also joined by Army regulars. A disaster was in the making.

Violence erupted with the protestors antagonizing the police, and the police, in turn, reacting with hostility to any perceived defiance: chanting by the protestors turned into police beatings and gassing. Senator Abe Ribicoff denounced the violence at the podium to which Richard Daley responded: his aides later explained that he had yelled, "Faker!" The violence also spilled into the auditorium jostling CBS reporter Dan Rather about while filming. As a result, arrests followed in Chicago, and trials ensued.

The Chicago Seven began as the Chicago Eight. Black Panther Bobby Seale continually disrupted the proceedings (the judge had him gagged and bound to a chair) and as a result, Judge Hoffman severed him from the trial and gave him a four-year sentence for contempt. This left seven defendants: Abbie Hoffman (no relation to the judge), Jerry Rubin, Tom Hayden, Rennie Davis, David Dellinger, John Froines, and Lee Wiener.

The defendants mocked the trial with continual antics. The seven were acquitted of conspiracy but convicted of crossing state lines with the intention to incite a riot at the DNC. Eventually, the convictions were overturned on the basis of a biased judge. No retrials occurred.

Despite the distractions, the Chicago convention did conduct business and nominated Hubert H. Humphrey. During the fall, he led a losing campaign against Richard Nixon, the Republican nominee. Johnson would die four short years after leaving the White House. The New Deal Coalition crashed to an inglorious end.


## VIETNAM AND CONSTITUTIONAL CHANGES

*After allowing President Johnson full reign in Southeast Asia through the Tonkin Gulf Resolution, and the resulting disaster, Congress decided to reclaim its authority in declaring and conducting war. In 1973 the War Powers Act restricted some presidential ability in the role of commander-in-chief. The changes included: a reassertion of Congressional authority to declare war, presidential reporting to Congress when using armed forces, and a time limitation of military actions unless extended by Congress.*

~ 119 ~

Congress had utterly capitulated to the executive in 1964, and the result became the War in Vietnam that completely turned the decade upside down. In that pivotal year, Congress passed the Tonkin Gulf Resolution opening the door for Johnson to escalate the war in Vietnam. The ramp-up came after the election; during the election, LBJ made the statement, "I don't think American boys should be in Asia doing what Asian boys should be doing for themselves." Although he portrayed himself as a reluctant warrior, his campaign painted a picture of Republican opponent Barry Goldwater as a dangerous warmonger. Johnson won the presidential election in a landslide.

In 1965, American planes bombed North Vietnam as the Vietcong increased attacks in South Vietnam (Operation Rolling Thunder would continue into 1968). Ho Chi Minh rejected negotiation talks. Johnson began to "Americanize" the war: the troop presence would rise every year until reaching its peak in 1969, swelling from 180,000 American troops in 1966 to a maximum of 540,000 in 1969. Although student protests on college campuses rose during the mid-Sixties, Johnson kept the majority of Americans on his side as he claimed slow but steady success in the war.

The American soldiers could not effectively engage their opponents face-to-face, so they used their superior mobility, helicopters, to take an area, "cleanse" it, and retreat. Of course, this meant that they did not physically control that area, a situation that certainly had to be frustrating to troops and spilled over into action, the most notable occurring at My Lai. In 1968, American planes bombed North Vietnamese trails into the south and Vietcong supply bases in Laos and Cambodia. The devastating blow to American morale came in January, however, with the Tet Offensive.

North Vietnamese troops poured into the south on the Vietnamese new year. Americans and South Vietnamese were caught off guard and took some time to organize a resistance. American news cameras were rolling all the time and portrayed the event as an American defeat, and the public went with the news services. Ironically, the North ultimately suffered a colossal defeat losing about two-thirds of its military capability. The problem, the Americans and the South Vietnamese never followed up on this infliction of damage. As a result, public opinion began to turn against "Johnson's war," and he would not gain reelection.

~ 120 ~

As Johnson's successor, Richard Nixon inherited Vietnam and worked hard to extricate American troops from Southeast Asia. As he struggled, Congress decided to stand up and reclaim some of its authority. The War Powers Act of 1973 placed some framework on presidential action. The law contains several provisions:

- Presidential military action must be as a result of a declaration of war by Congress, Congressional authority to use force, or a national emergency stemming from an attack from an invader.
- The president is required to report to Congress if armed force is deployed.
- Military actions are limited to 60 days unless extended by Congress, or Congress is physically unable to meet because of an invasion.

Nixon vetoed the bill, but Congress overrode the veto. Although tested by presidents, the law remains as an executive restraint today.

### *ROE V. WADE*: **THE AMERICAN POLITICAL DIVISION MANIFESTED IN LAW**

*The issue of abortion is contentious by its nature, and the decision in* Roe v. Wade *has not dampened this divide. It took several years to construct the Roe argument based on a concept of the right to privacy, and this period stretched from the mid-1960s to the Roe decision of 1973 (although the Roe case actually began in 1969). In essence, the argument became, how far does the interest of the state in preserving life go to overriding personal freedom? The Roe decision tried to hang this on the concept of viability outside the womb but has failed to satisfy any interest group or political perspective. In fact, this may have been the issue that ushered in the age of constitutional contention to accompany the dissolution of the New Deal political coalition.*

Making our last stop in our time travel, in 1973, we find the US to be a very different place from where we began. At this point, the federal government is accepted as a daily part of everybody's life. Regulations are pervasive, taxes are also daily, and everyone points to the Constitution as supporting their policy position. Expecting a new

Insidious Changes

document, we find the 1787 version with only a few amendments. Wow, what a difference interpretation makes!

We are at the point in time when interpretation is about to become socially contentious. In 1973, the Supreme Court decision of *Roe v. Wade* ignited political opposition often not seen in the US. The decision will cause some voters to switch political candidates and then party loyalties, hold annual rallies in Washington, DC, develop new politically active organizations centered on religion, and cause Supreme Court justice nominees to be subjected to public character assassination. The world of two Americas is about to be a reality.

In our minds, let's return to the analogy of the engine and replacing diesel as fuel rather than the required gasoline. We realize that for many years, policymakers have been substituting their beliefs for the written document of the Constitution. Nowhere in the Constitution does it call for the federal government to be the regulatory, administrative state it has become. Nowhere does it call for diminishing the power of the states in domestic politics. Nowhere does it call for justices making policy in place of legislators, but yet, here we are at this point in our trip. An engine can be converted to use a different type of fuel, but it requires deliberate construction to complete the makeover. If not, and we continually place the wrong fuel in the engine, it is only a matter of time until the engine falters. The Constitution has an amendment process that allows for changes, for allowing more federal power, but this approach is usually avoided. Instead, various policymakers continue to ask the system to do the exact opposite of what it was designed to do. How long can this continue without significant damage? Well, we are on the verge of our answer, and the cracks of abuse will appear with a court decision, a decision that causes huge public demonstrations from both sides, even decades after the verdict became public.

In 1821, Connecticut passed the first law to restrict abortion, and by 1900 every state had some type of restrictive abortion statute. However, with the changing social standards and mores of the 1960s, the Court began to reinterpret reproduction rights, most notably in *Griswold v. Connecticut* (1965). In the Griswold decision, the Court struck down state restrictions on the use of contraceptives by a married couple 7-2 with most of the opinions hinging on the 5th, 9th, and 14th Amendments, setting the stage for the Roe decision.

Insidious Changes

Norma McCorvey found herself pregnant with her third child during 1969, and more than once attempted to have an abortion. Texas law thwarted all these attempts, and McCorvey eventually filed a lawsuit in the US District Court of North Texas. The district court struck down the Texas restrictions based mostly on the 9th Amendment argument. Of course, the case quickly went to appeal, but it took a few years before the case reached the Supreme Court.

Finally, in 1973, the Court rendered its decision upholding the district court ruling on the basis of privacy, but with less emphasis on the 9th Amendment. Writing for the majority, Justice Harry Blackmun constructed a continuum of private rights as opposed to the state's right to protect and preserve life. He developed his logic based on trimesters of pregnancy, with the first being mostly the choice of the mother, but with the interest of the state becoming increasingly compelling as the new life moved to independent viability, considered at the time to be mostly in the third trimester. The decision immediately became subject to criticism.

Opponents find the Roe decision to be the worst example of judicial activism.[62] The Declaration of Independence, the founding document of the US, unequivocally states that we have an inherent right to "life, liberty, and the pursuit of happiness." When privacy is mentioned in the Constitution, it is in specific terms, such as the 4th Amendment:

> The right of the people to be secure in their persons, houses, papers, and effects, against unreasonable searches and seizures, shall not be violated, and no Warrants shall issue, but upon probable cause, supported by Oath or affirmation, and particularly describing the place to be searched, and the persons or things to be seized.

However, abortion is not usually argued in terms of constitutional language, but rather on the emotional terms of the mother's rights as opposed to life vs. death. Traditionally, police powers, such as the health, safety, and welfare of citizens, had been the purview of the

---

[62] This brings up the argument of *stare decisis*, Latin for let the decision stand. Proponents argue that years of legal reasoning can be overturned by a recent decision., such as occurred in the Brown decision of 1954. However, too much of this type of reasoning can threaten precedent and make the law capricious.

Insidious Changes

states, but Roe overturned state restrictions on abortion. In the end, it should be noted that the decision has developed into a political wedge that has separated conservatives from liberals. With that said, the ruling has undergone many changes since its inception.

In the Casey decision of 1992, the Court placed more emphasis on the individual's rights as opposed to the interests of the state, and also on viability with medical assistance versus true functional independence. The decision became even more controversial in 1995 when McCorvey began to speak out against the decision and continued her pro-life advocacy until her death in 2017. Each year a March for Life is held in front of the Supreme Court building to protest the decision. The controversy continues into the present as state legislatures have been passing increasingly restrictive statutes to be tested in court.

## DID RICHARD NIXON USHER IN A CONSERVATIVE ERA?

*Among presidential legacies, that of Richard Nixon is undoubtedly complicated and detailed. Considered to have been a master of foreign policy, he irritated many liberals with his tactics designed to reach a suitable exit from Vietnam. However, he delighted them with two other accomplishments: the recognition of the People's Republic of (Red) China, and a policy of détente (living with) toward the Soviet Union, proved to be steps that the liberal political establishment would enthusiastically applaud. However, Nixon's always blustery personality, and his previous tenure on the House Un-American Activities Committee (HUAC) kept him as a target for many of the Washington insiders. He would butt heads with Congress and the media several times, losing significant battles in court over the so-called Pentagon Papers and prompting Congress to pass the Impoundment Control Act of 1974 to force the president to distribute funds for congressionally approved public programs. In the end, no matter what his inclinations may have been, he served as president in a time when liberals held considerable power. As a result, Nixon tended to work within politically defined parameters he influenced, but did not necessarily construct.*

~ 124 ~

Richard Nixon entered Congress in 1946, became famous as a member of the House Un-American Activities Committee (HUAC), which investigated the penetration of the federal bureaucracy by Soviet spies, the Second Red Scare precipitated by Wisconsin Senator Joe McCarthy. He doggedly pursued Alger Hiss in the State Department and played an instrumental role in turning up the Pumpkin Papers of Whitaker Chambers, revealing State Department correspondence to the Soviets. Alger Hiss would eventually go to prison for two years, but not for spying. Instead, Hiss went to prison for lying to Congress rather than espionage (because the statute of limitations expired). Of course, all of this occurred at the same time as the Rosenberg's execution for espionage (passing atom secrets to the Soviets).[63]

Nixon would serve two terms as vice president to Dwight Eisenhower (dodging a political bullet of corruption with the Checker's Speech), but then lost a very tight race to JFK in 1960. He returned to California for a while, but there he lost a bid for governor in 1962. Promising the press that they would no longer have Nixon to kick around, even being pronounced politically dead on national television, could not slay the political Nixon.

In 1968, Nixon broke his promise to the media and reemerged on the national political scene. He won the Republican nomination for president, and with his appeal to the Silent Majority, proceeded to win rather handily Democrat Hubert Humphrey (George Wallace ran as a third-party candidate and took five Southern states). However, victory can be a double-edged sword, and the cutting side for Nixon would be his inheritance of the war in Vietnam.

The war in Vietnam brought violence to every American TV every night. By the end of the decade, color television was the standard: almost every American could watch the conflict in vivid, color reality, images that brought the horror of war into near reality. Nixon inherited a war he did not want to lose but knew he had to end. He talked of "peace with honor," a goal he and his National Security

---

[63] In this controversial case and sentence, husband and wife Julius and Ethel Rosenberg were accused and convicted of spying for the Soviets and supplying them with atomic secrets. Today, the evidence seems to point to Julius being the spy and his wife Ethel having little knowledge of his activities.

Insidious Changes

Advisor Henry Kissinger, who would become Secretary of State in 1973, sought for most of Nixon's tenure in the White House.

Kissinger engaged the North Vietnamese in secret negotiations to end the conflict, but when the North walked away, Nixon renewed the bombing campaign of Hanoi and mined the harbor of Haiphong. Nixon would also order the invasion of Cambodia and Laos to shut down the stream of supplies from the north to the Vietcong. Student protests increased on college campuses ending in real tragedy, four dead, in April 1970 at Kent State University in Ohio. Eventually, Kissinger negotiated a cease-fire with North Vietnam in 1973, but the south fell two years later when Congress refused to appropriate more money to the effort. The team also pursued a foreign policy of détente, which brought the Strategic Arms Limitation Talks, eventually reducing the active nuclear arsenals of the United States and the Soviet Union. Also, the policy broke through on individual freedom with the Helsinki Agreement (signed after Nixon left office), which contained a Soviet acknowledgment of human rights in politics. This statement would become a wedge between the Soviets and Eastern Europeans during the 1980s. Finally, Nixon would also find some stability in the Middle East, but at a cost resulting in the 1973 oil embargo by Arab states.

Nixon is a very complicated president, breaking new ground in foreign policy, but also growing the federal government. He signed the legislation for the Clean Air Act, creating the Environmental Protection Agency, and also signed the bill to establish the Occupational Safety and Health Administration, he devalued the dollar against gold, and he would twice implement wage and price controls to control inflation (this worked for a while but helped fuel even higher rates of inflation in the latter part of the decade). He initiated the War on Drugs and the War on Cancer, but on the other hand, he deferred to the states by favoring block grants to be tailored by state and local governments for use in federal programs. He also proved to be a staunch opponent of Soviet expansion despite his policy of détente, agreed to the Anti-Ballistic Missile Treaty, and promoting cooperation between the two space rivals. Nixon would also inadvertently set some constitutional markers.

The Pentagon Papers found their way to the New York Times in 1971, and the Nixon administration sought to block publication of the secret documents. The Times went to court and eventually won a

Supreme Court decision that the papers had entered the public realm and could not be barred from printing. He also vetoed the Clean Water Act because he believed the price tag to be too high. Congress overrode the veto, but Nixon impounded the funds. Again he lost in federal and received an order to release all allocated funds. In 1974, Congress passed the Impoundment Control Act, so today all vagueness is gone: the president cannot withhold allocated funds.

Nixon is a complicated study. He used political developments to his advantage and proved successful many times. He set some important constitutional precedents, but not intentionally. His ever contentious relationship with the press always kept him in the political spotlight, and usually in an unfavorable light. However, all previous negative press paled in comparison to the reports of the Watergate scandal.

## THE WATERGATE SCANDAL AND ITS RESULTING FALLOUT

*"It's not the crime, it's the cover-up" is an old adage that applies to the Watergate scandal. No one could put the finger on Nixon for the break-in to the Democrat National Headquarters, but they did connect the president to the cover-up. Attempting to keep himself out of controversy, Nixon wound up being the only president ever to resign, a move that came to prevent a nearly inevitable impeachment and removal from office.*

The Nixon administration met its demise over a break-in that seemed to be a minor criminal footnote when it occurred. The conclusion, however, proved to be anything but minor.

The White House became concerned about the number of leaks emanating from the administration (especially after the publication of the *Pentagon Papers*), so a special group was formed to plug these leaks: they became known as the Plumbers. The group effectively achieved its goals until June 1972: working under the organization that became known as CREEP (Committee to Reelect the President), the Plumbers broke into Democrat National Headquarters. Caught and arrested, the group of five received orders to keep mum, and they did, but the judge threatened them with a harsh sentence if they did

~ 127 ~

not cooperate. Finally, James McCord wrote a letter to Judge Sirica explaining a broader set of players. The chase was on!

Nixon managed to keep the lid on episode until after the fall election: the Washington *Post* journalists Bob Woodward and Carl Bernstein persisted in their investigation, and in May 1973, the Democrat-controlled Senate began hearings with Sam Ervin of North Carolina presiding. Top White House aides denied the administration's involvement until they reached Special Counsel John Dean. The drama increased.

Nixon had appointed Archibald Cox as a special prosecutor for the Watergate matter in May 1973. In Senate hearings, it had been revealed that Nixon taped conversations in the Oval Office. Cox pursued these tapes with vigor, but Nixon refused to turn them over. In October, Nixon fired Cox and replaced him with Leon Jaworski. The Attorney General and the next highest official in the Department of Justice (DOJ) resigned in protest of the move, an event labeled by the press as the Saturday Night Massacre.

To make matters worse, the DOJ accused Vice President Spiro Agnew of kickbacks while governor of Maryland, and alleged he continued this practice as VP. He ultimately resigned, and Nixon appointed Congressman Gerald Ford of Michigan in his place as provided for under the newly adopted Twenty-fifth Amendment.

In November, Nixon defended himself with a memorable comment, "The people have the right to know if their president is a crook. Well, I am not a crook." In April 1974, Nixon reluctantly handed over seven of the nine tapes subpoenaed to Sirica. Two, Nixon explained, did not exist, and one contained an 18 ½ minute gap. By July, Nixon faced impeachment on three counts from the House of Representatives. On August 5, Nixon resigned: when he climbed aboard his presidential helicopter, he flashed victory signs before flying off to his home in California only to be heard from again three years later when he appeared in a series of interviews with David Frost. During the interview, he lamented his regrets of what could have been, and that if the president takes action for matters of national security, "it is not illegal" by its nature.

## THE LEMON TEST AND RELIGION

*The Lemon Test is a three-prong approach to determining if the*

Insidious Changes

*religious provisions of the 1st Amendment have been violated. The Court released its ruling in 1971, and the test is still used today in 1st Amendment cases.*

With inflation rapidly threatening the affordability of school instructional materials, the states of Pennsylvania and Rhode Island offered programs to subsidize these purchases. Subsidies were offered to parochial schools, and lawsuits were filed based on the states favoring religious instruction. Conflicting decisions at the circuit level led the Supreme Court to combine and hear the cases from these two states.

In the ruling delivered in 1973, the Court used a three-prong test to determine the extent of governmental involvement in religion.

- The policy must have a clear, secular legislative purpose (Purpose Prong).
- The policy must not either promote or inhibit religion (Effect Prong).
- There must not be excessive entanglement of government with religion (Entanglement Prong).

In this case, the Court ruled that the legislature did indeed have a secular purpose, providing for education, not the promotion of religion. The Court made no judgment on the second prong but ruled against the policy based on the third prong. The decision held that schools were an integral part of the Catholic Church, and the statute did indeed constitute excessive entanglement as the state monies would help perpetuate the parochial schools. Having failed one of the prongs, the Court overturned using public funds in religious schools.

In the 1997 case of *Agostini v. Felton,* the court ruled that the entanglement prong should not be independent but rather in consideration of the other two factors, so the test has been modified. An opposing theory to the Lemon Test advocates using coercion and endorsement tests in place of the three prongs. Again, the controversy continues.

## EXECUTIVE ORDER 11905 AND ITS IMPACT ON THE CIA

*In December 1974, the New York* Times *broke a story about CIA*

Insidious Changes

*domestic operations, which triggered congressional and executive reviews. In the end, Richard Nixon's successor Gerald Ford issued EO 11905 to provide stronger oversight of covert operations and end the assassination of foreign leaders.*

Watergate had many ramifications, one being the attempt of President Nixon to dismantle and reorganize the Central Intelligence Agency in his favor after the break-in. The Nixon administration attempted to shift blame for the hotel burglary to the CIA in an attempt to deflect blame onto the organization, weaken it, and then reform it in his image as he believed it had become rouge and self-perpetuating.

To coordinate intelligence efforts during World War II, FDR authorized the formation of the Organization of Strategic Services (OSS) based on the British model of information gathering (the agency known as MI6). After the war, the National Security Act of 1947 established the Central Intelligence Agency (CIA) to perform the civilian functions of the then defunct OSS. Truman approached the agency with caution, but Eisenhower embraced its possibilities. With Allen Dulles in charge of the CIA and his brother John Foster Dulles heading up the State Department, covert operations became the go-to in many international situations. However, much of this period consisted of assassinating or replacing foreign leaders. Iran, Guatemala, Syria, Indonesia, and the Congo all made the list for targeting before Gary Powers went down over the Soviet Union while photographing strategic installations. These activities, combined with failures in Cuba, especially the Bay of Pigs, brought down the reputation of the clandestine organization. As these covert operations became public knowledge during the late 1960s, reform calls began to increase.

Shortly after Nixon's reelection, he replaced CIA Director Richard Helms with James Schlesinger implementing his plan to downsize the agency. Schlesinger conducted an internal investigation, fired a significant number of agents, and collected a bevy of information concerning covert operations, a collection that became known as the Family Jewels.

Within the Family Jewels were a collection of operations including mind control attempts (including the use of the hallucinogenic lysergic acid diethylamide-LSD) in Project MKUltra, assassinations

~ 130 ~

of foreign leaders, and surveillance of American citizens in Operation CHAOS.  The Family Jewels would be leaked to the press.

The New York *Times* broke the story in late 1975.  In response, Gerald Ford (Nixon's replacement as president) established the Rockefeller Commission (now vice president) to investigate CIA activity and Congressional hearings also began with the Church and Pike committees (chaired by Senator Frank Church and Rep. Otis Pike, respectively).  In the end, Ford issued EO 11905 to provide stronger oversight of covert operations and end the assassination of foreign leaders.  The Pike Committee's work established rules for oversight and declassification.  Church's work put a heavy wall between domestic and international surveillance, a move that critics claimed hindered the US in gathering intelligence concerning the 9/11 attack of 2001 (see below).

## THE EQUAL RIGHTS AMENDMENT: DEAD OR ALIVE?

*An Equal Rights Amendment has been a long-standing issue in American politics, stretching back nearly a century.  The last ERA, although expired, passed out of Congress in 1972, failed to be ratified, but fomented a great deal of social controversy in public debate.*

In 1963, Betty Friedan published *The Feminine Mystique* challenging the female role of the housewife in American society as unsatisfying, beginning a reform movement.  Friedan formed the National Organization for Women (NOW) in 1966, and in essence, gave foundational support to the Second Feminist Movement (the first ending with the 19th Amendment).  In advocating for the removal of the traditional role of women, NOW made a significant public impact in September 1968 at the Miss America Pageant, where they joined other women's groups and "burned their bras" as a sign of throwing off the restrictions of society.  Because of its contentious nature, the Roe decision did little to unite women politically.  However, NOW persisted and endorsed the ERA.

Much like Roe, the ERA of 1972 also generated much debate concerning its benefits and limitations.  The opposition argument usually came in the form that by law, women had certain specific

~ 131 ~

rights at the workplace (they were a protected class), and the proposed ERA would remove these much-needed protections. The proponents and opponents came and went over the years, but organized labor tended to remain opposed. Part of the idea of ERA equality passed in the Civil Rights Act of 1964, which included a ban on employment discrimination based on sex. However, in 1971 Representative Martha Griffiths of Michigan revived the effort, and the following year the resolution made it through Congress and headed to the states. The ERA contained a "sunset clause," as many amendment proposals do, which seemed not to matter at first, but became a point of contention later. Although ratification seemed to take off like a rocket, Phyllis Schlafly became an ardent opponent and slowed its passage.

A longtime conservative activist, Schlafly argued against the ERA based on loss of privilege. Women could potentially lose the right to separate bathrooms, military exemptions, and other special considerations for women. Although ERA sailed through 28 states, it began to stall and only had 35 states when the original sunset became effective on March 22, 1979. In 1978, Congress had passed a joint resolution attempting to extend the deadline into 1982, but no more states ratified the amendment. In fact, five tried to rescind their ratifications before or at the original deadline. Since the 1980s, Nevada (2017), Illinois (2018), and finally Virginia in 2020 became the 38th state to ratify the dead amendment. The amendment has stirred many emotions, did little to unite women, and in 2020 became a symbol of the left ignoring previously revered protocol in an attempt to make their policies law through all means necessary.

## AFFIRMATIVE ACTION AND THE BAKKE DECISION

*The Great Society included LBJ's executive order (EO 10925) to provide preferential treatment for non-white students when applying to universities. Allan Bakke applied several times to medical schools, but despite excellent academic achievement, he would be denied while minority students were accepted. Finally, Bakke went to court and won in California, but the US Supreme Court set this decision aside and agreed to hear the case. In a 5-4 decision, the Court ruled in favor of adding minority status as a plus in applications but rejected institutional quotas.*

Marine veteran Allan Bakke left Vietnam and the military to achieve his master's in engineering. Bakke decided upon medical school, scored high on the Medical College Examination Test (MCAT), and applied to the University of California-Davis. However, his application would be rejected.

The University of California-Davis opened a medical school in 1968 with a focus on minorities. With this mission, the school set aside a percentage of its admissions for non-white students. So, the program would be well-established when Bakke applied in 1972.

After Bakke's initial rejection, he waited a year and applied to several more colleges along with UC-Davis, only to meet rejection on all attempts. Contemplating a lawsuit, Bakke waited another year before again being turned down by UC-Davis. Bakke had reached the end of his patience.

Bakke's lawsuit cited violations of Title VI of the 1964 Civil Rights Act and equal protection under the 14th Amendment. The process ended with the California Supreme Court siding with Bakke in a decisive 6-1 decision. However, the US Supreme Court set this verdict aside and moved to hear the case. The *University of California Board of Regents v. Bakke* became one of the most critical decisions from the court during the 1970s.

The presidential administration of Jimmy Carter stood at a crossroad in its desire to champion affirmative action, but hesitant on the matter of quotas. The case drew a throng of *amicus* briefs on both sides, including the NAACP, the Anti-Defamation League, the American Jewish Congress, and the Congressional Black Caucus. The Carter administration filed its support for affirmative action, but opposition to quotas.

The final 5-4 decision from the Court stated that although the government had a compelling interest to have more minorities admitted to higher education, nowhere could the use of quotas find justification in the Constitution. The Court did accept the Harvard model of providing a plus for racial diversity while avoiding quotas. Bakke won his admission to UC-Davis, completed medical school, and entered the medical field. The case is considered to have accomplished much to alleviate reverse-discrimination, real or

~ 133 ~

Insidious Changes

potential, by providing consideration for past racial discrimination without applying hard numbers for acceptance that would exclude some races in favor of others.

# IX: THE CONSTITUTION IN THE ERA OF POLITICAL CONTENTION

## CONSERVATIVES UNITE: THE REAGAN REVOLUTION

*Ronald Reagan countered the Progressive reinterpretation of the Constitution, restoring relevancy to the states while allowing markets to bolster the American economy. His amiable personality, success in office, and hope for the future gave impetus to the conservative movement for years to follow.*

On January 20, 1981, Reagan gave his inaugural address, which set the tone for his presidency. "Government is not the solution to our problems; government is the problem," he firmly asserted. Federal Reserve Chairman Paul Volcker pushed a hard line on inflation, and the new president stayed with him. Reagan pushed through the Economic Tax Recovery Act of 1981 to reduce tax rates and stimulate the economy. The new policy, known as supply-side economics, won the day as the tax package proved to be the beginning of Reagan's successful efforts to revitalize the American economy.

Americans had suffered through a decade of economic stress and political turmoil. With Nixon's resignation, the only unelected vice president became our only unelected president. Ford led a nation fed up with Washington insiders and suffering from all types of economic dislocation. Inflation ate into their pocketbooks, and unemployment remained uncomfortably high. The Era of Malaise had taken root.

Economically, Americans struggled to tread water during the 1970s. They sought another answer to business as usual in Washington. The electorate thought they had a solution in Jimmy Carter, but his policies proved ineffective. As Carter struggled, a political movement began to form, the New Right. Evangelical Christians, Pro-Life activists, the Neo-Conservative movement (the intellectuals who sought a strong America and more market solutions for the economy), and average workers feeling the squeeze of turbulent global change came together seeking another solution.

Ronald Reagan warmly embraced the New Right and told all Americans they could do better. His optimism won the day in the

~ 135 ~

1980 election and won him reelection in 1984. The American economy, and American world leadership, both recovered under the actor, turned spokesman, turned politician. Americans began to leave behind the pessimism of the Seventies and pick up the Reagan optimism. As Reagan would later run in his reelection advertisements, "It's morning again in America."

When Ronald Reagan took office in 1981, the presidency had been plagued with scandal and weakness; when he left, the office had regained respect in the US and around the world. The economic expansion that began under his administration persisted for many years. Much of this came from deregulation (begun under Carter, and accelerated under Reagan), and the emphasis on high-technology development.

Reagan redefined American politics. The Republican Party identifies itself with Reagan to this day. He is an icon because of his popularity, his attraction of moderate voters, and his articulation of conservatism. However, the Reagan Revolution did not happen overnight or all by itself. The conservative leader at first met opposition from other conservatives, a lot of negative press coverage, especially on his economic approach, and almost continual opposition to his foreign policy until the fall of the Soviet Union. Despite all this, Reagan's policies prevailed, and he is still associated with a prosperous economy and a strong global presence for the US.

Reagan implemented conservative economic policies focused on growing production rather than increased spending. Reagan cut taxes, and the economy grew. His economic impact is clear when placed in the cold, hard light of facts. As calculated by Louis D. Johnston and Samuel H. Williamson, the GDP (gross domestic product, the sum of all goods and services produced within the US for a given year) rose from the 1982 recession level of $3.3 trillion to $5.5 trillion in 1989 (in 2000 dollars). The beginning mark in 1976 would be $1.825 trillion. If we follow this out to 1993, the last year of Bush I's budget, the GDP had climbed to $6.6 trillion.

If we place this data in individual terms, we get a bit clearer picture. The per capita GDP grew in the following manner (in 2000 dollars):

- 1976    $19,961
- 1982    $22,346
- 1989    $28,221

~ 136 ~

From 1976 through 1982, the GDP annually grew $477 per capita, whereas from 1982 to 1989, it jumped $734.38 per year: not a bad increase, and with decreasing inflation!

Here's how the supply-side economics policy worked: as the tax burden decreased on those with investment capital, the incentive to invest increased. This investment increased efficiency and output, which made more goods available at a lower price; at a lower price, more goods are sold. As more goods are sold, the more jobs are created to produce the goods. In fact, during Reagan's tenure in office, the American economy created 16 million new jobs. Inflation also fell dramatically to 4.13 percent in 1989 from its double-digit heights at the end of Carter's tenure.

Reagan's opponents labeled his policy "trickle-down economics," asserting that his policies made the wealthy wealthier and only a bit trickled down to those of lesser income. True, Reagan's policy of limited government corralled spending on Medicaid, food stamp programs, and other social programs other than Social Security or Medicare. Even the mention of modifications here brought such a backlash of public opinion that Reagan immediately abandoned any follow-up proposals.

Reagan's policy ended price controls on domestic oil and eventually repealed the Windfall profit tax on oil (1988) that had driven oil production offshore. Since this action, the US economy has not suffered the type of oil shortages seen in the 1970s.

In his farewell address, Reagan voiced his regret that the national debt had grown (from $700 billion to $3 trillion). However, his paltry $3 trillion debt is now north of an enormous $22 trillion (and running exponentially higher with the COVID-19 economic countermeasures), and consumer credit card debt is $900 billion, and student loans exceed this amount. Is Reagan to blame, or are Americans hooked on easy credit and easy, short-term solutions?

Historically, Americans prefer low taxes. Although the USSR, the great rival of the US, collapsed under his watch, George H. W. Bush lost his reelection bid at least partly because he reneged on his ". . . no new taxes" promise, trusting the Democrat leadership of Congress by giving them a tax increase in exchange for the promise of decreased spending. In December 2018, when Bush's coffin was loaded into the hearse for his final trip from Capitol Hill where he had been lying in state, that spending decrease had not yet developed.

~ 137 ~

When President Clinton took office, he worked with Congress to raise taxes and promptly lost Congress to the Republicans in the off-year election.  It seems that as a nation, we want all types of services, but we do not want to pay for them.

## BORKING: HOW A SUPREME COURT NOMINEE BECOME AN ENDURING SYMBOL OF POLITICAL CONTENTION

*A noun became a verb in the 1980s when President Reagan had an opportunity to select a Supreme Court justice.  To be Borked became synonymous with a successful public assault on a political figure. This system has continued to this day when conservative nominees are sent to the Senate for approval: the most prominent examples would be the nominations hearings of Clarence Thomas (1991) and Brett Kavanaugh (2018), both accused of sexual misconduct during their confirmation proceedings.*

Politicians can come and go, they must stand for election at a specified time, and often executives are term-limited.  However, Supreme Court justices can remain on the bench for decades handing down policy decisions that carry the effect of law (known as public law, i.e., *Brown v. Board of Education* and *Roe v. Wade*).  As a result, the political stakes have become very high: it all started with Robert Bork's nomination in 1987 and his position on abortion.

When Associate Justice Lewis Powell announced his retirement in the summer of 1987, President Reagan nominated conservative judge Robert Bork for the high court.  In response, Massachusetts Senator Ted Kennedy effectively launched a media attack to provide a one-sided profile of a nominee opposed to the senator's judicial ideology. The attack was one step away from character assassination, which has become a fixture of American politics today: attacks that tend to be void of any balanced reporting or investigation.  In the case of Bork, a full career provided plenty of fodder for the opposition.

Bork's public image took a hit in the 1970s.  At the height of the Watergate Scandal, President Nixon ordered his Attorney General Eliot Richardson to fire Special Prosecutor Archibald Cox.  Cox had ordered Nixon to hand over the White House tapes of Oval Office conversations, and Nixon retaliated decisively. However, Richardson resigned rather than comply with the president's order. The Deputy Attorney General William Ruckelshaus also resigned rather than fire Cox. The duty then fell on Solicitor General Robert Bork, who pulled the trigger and completed the Saturday Night Massacre (the firing came over the weekend). The media headlines became enflamed and portrayed Nixon as a power-hungry, out of control near-dictator tearing apart the Constitution to destroy American democracy. Fast forward 15 years.

President Reagan nominated Bork to replace retiring Supreme Court Justice Lewis Powell. As noted above, Massachusetts Senator, and arch-liberal, Ted Kennedy, immediately sprang into action. In a press conference Kennedy unleashed a vicious attack:

> Robert Bork's America is a land in which women
> would be forced into back-alley abortions, blacks
> would sit at segregated lunch counters, rogue police
> could break down citizens' doors in midnight raids,
> schoolchildren could not be taught about evolution,
> writers and artists could be censored at the whim of the
> Government, and the doors of the Federal courts would
> be shut on the fingers of millions of citizens for whom
> the judiciary is, and is often the only, protector of the
> individual rights that are the heart of our democracy . .
> . President Reagan . . . should not be able to . . . impose
> his reactionary vision of the Constitution on the
> Supreme Court and the next generation of Americans.
> No justice would be better than this injustice.

The swift attack proved devastating. Even the president's party turned on Bork, and the nominee could never reverse the tide. He faced constant attacks from the left concerning his stance on *Roe v. Wade*. Bork made no apologies for the fact that he did not believe that the Constitution held an implied right to privacy, the foundation of the Roe decision. After brutal hearings, the Senate finally took up a vote on Bork's nomination: Bork failed to be confirmed with 58 voting against him. Reagan would eventually nominate Anthony Kennedy to the highest bench as the replacement for Bork.

Did Borking have a political outcome? Yes, Kennedy became a critical swing vote throughout his tenure on the Court. He would be instrumental in *Planned Parenthood v. Casey,* which expanded the

Insidious Changes

role of the state in abortion cases, and *Citizens United v. FEC* concerning campaign expenditures by corporations. In these cases, he sided with conservatives. However, he certainly left the right in *Lawrence v. Texas* and *Obergefell v. Hodges* paving the road for legalized homosexuality and same-sex marriage. However, the Bork legacy lives on in how subsequent Court nominees are vetted.

When Thurgood Marshall (the Constitution is a living document) decided to retire in 1991, Clarence Thomas would also undergo the new treatment for a conservative justice nominee. After being accused of sexual misconduct by Anita Hill during his hearings, and delivering a blistering rebuke of Senate conduct over the treatment of his personal life, Thomas won a close vote 52-48. Later in 2018, Justice Kennedy's retirement brought another brutal hearing process for nominee Brett Kavanaugh. Although an ugly public process placed tempers at the boiling point, the vote again went in favor of confirmation.

As a result, Borked has become a verb for a successful public assault on a court nominee. Ted Kennedy effectively used the media to provide a one-sided attack that news organizations did little to investigate for balance. The Kavanaugh hearing demonstrated that Borking is alive and well, a sad reminder of the new heights of smear politics reached in 1987.

## BILL CLINTON: MODERATE TENDENCIES?

*Clinton's record as president would lead to the conclusion of no. Bill Clinton moved to the political center after the conservative backlash following his first two years as president, resulting in the Democrats losing Congress. However, with new Speaker Newt Gingrich at the helm in the House, Clinton signed legislation that fundamentally changed the nature of the American welfare state and has proven to be a lasting legacy from the Clinton era.*

A little known Congressman stood in front of the C-SPAN cameras many times during President Bill Clinton's first two years. As the Clinton's faltered with their health care makeover plan (see Obamacare section below), Newt Gingrich, Congressman from Georgia, and Republican Whip[64] increasingly made the news. As the

Insidious Changes

1994 mid-term elections began to draw closer, the genius of Gingrich emerged and took the day.

In 1993, Clinton signed the Family Medical Leave Act requiring private businesses to maintain job openings for 12 weeks (unpaid) during a medical leave absence (George H. W. Bush had vetoed the plan twice). Clinton also reversed a bevy of previous policies, including:

- lifting Reagan and Bush restrictions on abortion services;
- reversing his campaign proposal for a middle-class tax cut and raising taxes on the wealthiest Americans (it did have cuts for low-income individuals and small business);
- signed the gun purchase restrictions of the Brady Bill;
- and implemented the "Don't Ask, Don't Tell" policy for gay military personnel after significant bipartisan pushback on his proposal for all-out gay acceptance in the service branches (Congress would remove "Don't Ask, Don't Tell" in 2011).

Finally, he pursued health care reform, putting a task force under the leadership of his wife, Hillary Clinton. Hillary's plan to overhaul American medical coverage and implement a type of national health care met heavy opposition from Republicans, the American Medical Association, and the insurance industry. Clinton biographer John F. Harris blamed poor coordination within the White House for its failure to move the proposal successfully through the legislative process; however, the nearly year-long secrecy of the task force did not lend the proposal to a public feel of transparency. Even a modified version could not be ushered through by Senate Majority Leader George Mitchell, and as a result, the effort died.

Sensing blood in the water with the vulnerability of the Democrat Party after the Clinton fiasco of healthcare reform, the Republicans only needed a solid rallying point to overturn the House majority. Gingrich, along with Dick Armey, took this as a challenge and developed the "Contract with America," policy points the Republicans promised to hold votes on if they took control of the House. This plan to nationalize the Congressional election proved to

---

[64] Gingrich gained leadership as he became a founding member of the House Conservative Opportunity Society, which carried clout with President Reagan, and as he opposed Democrat House Speaker Jim Wright over Wright's book deal that seemed to skirt around political ethics reporting.

Insidious Changes

be the turning point. It redefined American government in the wake of a massive legislative turnover: 54 House seats and eight Senate seats, to gain complete Republican control of Congress, the first time in four decades.

As Gingrich ascended to leadership, the Republicans took votes and made some very important reforms, such as applying all new laws to Congressional members as well as the public. Applying a significant impact for the first time since 1980, when Congress reined in the bureaucracy with the Paper Work Reduction Act,[65] Congress took on the administrative state. With new Congressional leadership and a push from the National Governors Association, the Unfunded Mandate Act came into being. The new Republican Congress also passed the Congressional Review Act of 1996 as a check on bureaucratic regulation. Any regulation worth an annual economic impact of $100 million has a 60 day period of delay. During the delay, any House or Senate member may file a resolution of disapproval, which must go through committee, but if it makes it to the floor, it is fast-tracked to move through the 60-day window. If passed, it is subject to signature or veto from the president, and a veto can also be overridden under normal procedure. Amounts under $100 million automatically go into effect but can be repealed within 60 days under these procedures. Other laws included a presidential line-item veto to help balance the federal budget, stiffer criminal penalties, tax reform for married couples, and the loser pays in cases of lawsuit filings, which Clinton promptly vetoed.[66] In contrast to these reforms, the 104th Congress failed to enact term limits for Congress but did achieve a momentous change in 1996 with welfare reform.

---

[65] The Paper Work Reduction Act established the Office of Information and Regulatory Affairs within the Office of Management and Budget to scrutinize all new documents gathering information from ten or more people. The OIRA has the authority to block most unreasonable regulatory requirements.

[66] Several other Congressional attempts at fiscal constraint have failed, including the notable Gramm-Rudman-Hollings, by Senators Phil Gramm (R-TX), Warren Rudman (R-NH), and Fritz Hollings (D-SC) in the 1980s, which tried to pass off the balancing responsibility to the president. The line-item veto eventually went down to a Supreme Court decision declaring it unconstitutional. Today, an Article V effort is underway as a result of Washington failures. The Article V convention would give the task to the states to formulate a balanced budget amendment and the opportunity for its ratification.

~ 142 ~

President Clinton vetoed the first welfare reform bill sent to his desk. Congress came back with another proposal, the Personal Responsibility, and Work Opportunity Reconciliation Act, and this version became the bill signed into law by Clinton on August 22, 1996. The new law ended the cash program of Aid to Families with Dependent Children and replaced it with Temporary Assistance to Needy Families consisting of a workfare provision: to receive government benefits, the recipient must work or enter a job skill training program either with low or no pay which made the participant eligible for benefits. The benefits also had a time limit designed to encourage gainful employment (the Obama administration loosened some of these requirements during 2012 and the lagging recovery from the Great Recession, but Donald Trump quickly began to abandon the changes of his predecessor). In this policy realm, the conservative movement made an impact that continues over two decades after its passage.

## THE USA PATRIOT ACT'S IMPACT ON CONSTITUTIONAL RIGHTS

*In response to the attacks on September 9, 2001, and to track terrorist activities inside the US, Congress adopted the USA PATRIOT Act before the end of the year to detect terrorists within US borders and counter their activities. However, the law contained several provisions that run counter to the Bill of Rights, especially the protections within the 1st and 4th amendments. Edward Snowden, an intelligence contractor with the National Security Agency, blew the lid off of privacy concerns when he leaked classified documents in 2013, revealing the extent to which the NSA collected private information on American citizens. It also became controversial with its surveillance provisions through the Foreign Intelligence Service Act (FISA) courts during the 2016 presidential election.*

Splendid isolation refers to a situation of geography that benefits a country. The US enjoyed such a benefit for years having two wide oceans to the east and west, and having a sparsely populated neighboring country to the north, and a weak military opponent to the

Insidious Changes

south.  However, all this ended on the morning of September 11, 2001, with terrorist strikes on the US East Coast.

With the Soviet invasion of Afghanistan, oil sheik Osama bin-Laden formed Arab resistance.  After the First Gulf War (1991) and the continued presence of US troops in the Gulf region, bin-Laden began to call for a jihad to resist infidel aggression.  Bin-Laden's terrorist group al-Qaeda (formed 1988) became the organizing community of what would become a massive attack on American soil.

Although American authorities had warnings, such as the World Trade Center bombings of 1993, and an opportunity to eliminate bin-Laden (that Bill Clinton thwarted), the country was unprepared for the terrorist activity of September 11, 2001.  That bright, late summer morning as people filed into the World Trade Center to tend to their daily work, American Airlines Flight 11 hit the north tower.  Less than an hour later, a second plane, United Flight 175 hit the south tower.  Mass confusion hit as the towers caught on fire and eventually collapsed.  Following the World Trade Center strikes, American Airlines Flight 77 crashed into the Pentagon.  However, one terrorist crew took United Airlines Flight 93, intending to destroy the US Capitol, but failed when the passengers revolted, resulting in a crash in a distant Pennsylvania field.  Americans were shocked, the Stock Market shut down, the government went into their drills for a Cold War nuclear attack, and responses were planned.  Visiting Ground Zero in New York, President George W. Bush vowed that those responsible would pay, but first on the list of things to do would be the prevention of a similar, follow up attack.  The bureaucrats went to work.

The basic responses to 9/11 came with a reorganization of executive branch departments designed to increase cooperation in the detection of terrorist activity, and the addition of the Department of Homeland Security.  Also, the Department of Justice under Attorney General John Ashcroft proposed legislative changes to facilitate the detection of terrorist activity.  During the Clinton administration, the president had asked for more authority in tracking terrorists within the US, and Congress adopted a "light" version, but in 2001 such considered restraint fell by the wayside.

The Uniting and Strengthening America by Providing Appropriate Tools Required to Intercept and Obstruct Terrorism Act (USA PATRIOT Act) allowed the government, under Section 215, to

~ 144 ~

monitor American citizens in an effort to collect data on radical foreign operatives. This data included cell phones, emails, and provided for large data storage efforts to preserve information if needed to backtrack on suspected terrorists. This sweeping collection of data became a point of contention and eventually met revision.

The act has been revised several times and renewed once. Section 215 has been modified to prevent the collection of evidence from a general warrant, which is forbidden under the 4th Amendment. Also, the act has fallen into disrepute for its secrecy clauses. The revelations of Edward Snowden, a former intelligence service contractor concerning the extent of surveillance on American citizens by the National Security Agency, became a public media storm with his leaking of classified documents. Snowden's revelations piled on top of previous concerns and exposures concerning due process during the War on Terror.

The Bush administration had taken broad authority after 9/11. Subsequently, the extended detention of "enemy combatants" came under the scrutiny of the Court in several cases, including detainees Hamdi, Rasul, Hamdan, and Boumediene. These cases ranged from the rights of American citizens acting against their government to the extended lock-up of combatants, especially at Guantanamo Bay, the use of a military tribunal to prosecute terrorists and rights to *habeas corpus*. The courts modified some of the provisions in question, but the subsequent administration of Barack Obama circumvented a lot of the legal issues by using improved drone technology to eliminate enemy combatants in the field. However, some contention remains.

One very public controversy of the new surveillance rules included the use of the FISA court[67] during the presidential election of 2016. The documents submitted in support of the warrant must be sworn to by the submitting agents. Such documents were filed in a FISA court during the 2016 election cycle targeting the campaign team of Donald Trump. The filing used, the so-called Trump Dossier, a political hit piece produced to discredit the candidate.[68] The information within

---

[67] The PATRIOT Act provides for surveillance on American citizens to be authorized in a Foreign Intelligence Surveillance Act court, officially known as a Foreign Intelligence Surveillance Court, FISC.
[68] In current campaigns, candidate committees will conduct opposition research on their opponents seeking distasteful or questionable occurrences from the past. These events will then be used in a smear campaign of innuendo and distraction to

Insidious Changes

had little to no substantiating evidence, but yet resulted in the surveillance of Trump Tower and the Trump campaign team. After two years of investigation, the dossier would be publicly debunked in a special investigative report. However, despite all the issues surrounding the act, it has been renewed, albeit with modifications designed to give more protection to the average American.

## SIGNIFICANCE OF THE REHNQUIST COURT

*After several decades of the liberal interpretation of the Constitution as a "living" document to be read in the context of the jurists' time, the conservative majority court of Chief Justice William Rehnquist (strongly backed by Associate Justice Antonin Scalia) began to interpret the Constitution in terms of "originalist" interpretative approaches.[69] As a result, several High Court decisions began to restore the principles of a limited federal government.*

Conservatives have made an impact through appointments to the Supreme Court. Richard Nixon originally appointed William Rehnquist to the highest court in 1971. Rehnquist served as an associate justice until Warren Burger retired in 1986. President Reagan then nominated Rehnquist for Chief Justice, who eventually would be confirmed 65-33. His associate seat would be filled with fellow conservative Antonin Scalia. From 1986 until Rehnquist's death in 2005, the Court would restore constitutional authority to states and affirm state authority in criminal prosecutions.

The Rehnquist Court became known as a conservative court, often enhancing the states' role in federalism. In *US v. Lopez* (1995) the Rehnquist Court overturned statutes extending the commerce clause to allow federal laws restricting gun possession near schools. The Lopez decision served as the first push back from the Court on the commerce clause since the New Deal. (The ruling would be modified

---

negatively impact the opponent.

[69] Originalists are of two varieties, textualists and those favoring original intent. Textualists seek the meaning of the words within the statutes as they would be used by reasonable people of the time. Those seeking original intent try to discover the purpose of the legislation as intended by the drafters, often examining the debate of the legislators at the time of adoption.

to allow restrictions on guns that had moved through interstate commerce.) Also, *Printz v. US* would peel back some of the Brady Act purchasing requirements as running counter to the 10th Amendment. The 2000 decision in *US v. Morrison* would also roll back some Congressional extension of power under the commerce clause to include violent assault and rape actions against women.

Beyond federalism, Chief Justice Rehnquist also became heavily involved in politics. He became the second Chief Justice to preside over a presidential impeachment hearing in 1999 when the Senate tried President Clinton. In the 2000 presidential election, *Bush v. Gore* ended the contested results in Florida and declared George W. Bush the winner, a rare occasion when the popular vote did not match the Electoral College numbers. Florida became the swing vote, and the protracted recount morphed into slogans such as "hanging chads" that became part of the national dialogue. The decision halted a Florida Supreme Court manual recount partly based on the equal protection clause because different counties had differing standards for the recount.

Outside of federalism, the Rehnquist Court had a different tint and found an interesting split in the Court with *Texas v. Johnson*. During the Republican National Convention in Dallas during 1984, Gregory Lee Johnson burned a flag in protest of Ronald Reagan's policies. He was arrested and convicted under a Texas statute prohibiting the public desecration of the American flag, a law similar to 48 other states (many of them springing up after Vietnam protests). President George H. W. Bush, a World War II veteran, proposed to Congress that an amendment should be passed in light of the decision. Congress resisted and instead adopted the Flag Protection Act of 1989. However, the Court struck this statute down on the same grounds in 1990 with its decision in *US v. Eichman*. The Johnson ruling is odd in that liberal justices William Brennan, Hugh Blackmun, and Thurgood Marshall were joined by conservative Antonin Scalia and moderate Anthony Kennedy. Liberals John Paul Stevens and Byron "Whizzer" White along with conservative Sandra Day O'Connor rounded out those joining Rehnquist in opposition to the ruling.

In perhaps the second most famous case of the Rehnquist Court, at least at this juncture of history, *Lawrence v. Texas* (2003), the Chief Justice again found himself in the minority, this time along with

~ 147 ~

conservatives Scalia and Clarence Thomas. The Lawrence case overturned sodomy restrictions between consenting adults, even of the same sex. This decision ran counter to *Bowers v. Hardwick* (1986), which left such cases to the states. However, *Romer v. Evans* (1996) had begun to change this precedent as it provided a protected group based on sexual orientation under Colorado Amendment 2. Justice Kennedy wrote the majority opinion in this case, as well as *US v. Windsor* in 2013 that overturned the Defense of Marriage Act (DOMA) passed during the Clinton administration. After 28 states had adopted some type of referenda statute or amendment affirming traditional marriage, the Court had a well-defined social institution in its crosshairs. Finally, Kennedy tipped the scales and also wrote the 2015 majority opinion of *Obergefell v. Hodges,* which fully legalized same-sex marriage throughout the US, again citing the 14th Amendment.

## HOW OBAMACARE BECOME LAW

*Since the Fair Deal of Harry Truman, the Democrat Party has promoted universal, national health care. The Great Society serves as the high watermark of modern liberalism, and indeed President Lyndon Johnson instituted Medicare (for retirement-age Americans) and Medicaid (means-tested), but these fell short of universal coverage. The ineptitude of the Clinton administration nearly derailed the effort for good during the 1990s, but President Obama revived the initiative and pushed through a plan, dubbed Obamacare, during the first two years of his presidency. However, this far from settled the issue of universal health care.*

For years the matter of health care access has been a Washington issue. In the Fair Deal, Truman installed universal health care as a part of the Democrat Party platform, a plank that endures to this day. Pieces of health care reform have been accomplished, but the complete overhaul that the Democrats have sought remains a dream. In 2010, President Obama believed he had the opportunity to change this scenario, but he found the public to be resistant and caught a glimpse of why so many presidents before him struggled with the issue.

~ 148 ~

Although Harry Truman articulated the goal of universal health care in the US, he was not the first to propose the policy. Back in 1915, the Progressive Era, the American Association of Labor Legislation proposed insurance for workers, a bit short of Truman's belief in universal health care, but a serious proposal nonetheless. However, the policy died in the New York legislature, partly from the opposition of the medical profession. The proposal did not lay dormant for long and again found life in the 1920s with a mixture of several industry elements, only to be derailed by the Great Depression. The FDR administration would push a couple of times for universal health care, but ultimately these efforts would be dropped, one in favor of Social Security and the other, the Wagner National Health Care Act of 1939, found traction in Congress but suddenly found the shelf with the outbreak of World War II. However, group insurance, beginning in the Thirties with Blue Cross (hospitals) and Blue Shield (physicians), offered to companies and supplied to employees began to gain momentum. During wage and price controls of World War II these policies gained popularity to circumvent restrictions on gross wage increases. Company payments of premiums became a business deduction under Internal Revenue Service rules in 1951. Although the benefit of insurance became an employment benefit in American life, Harry Truman had visions of health care beyond the workplace.

Truman promoted the public discussion of universal health care, but unlike the British, the American cousins did not implement full national health care run by the government.[70] With the Cold War distractions of small theater wars and the Space Race, health care took a back seat. However, it would be the 1960s and LBJ before a policy breakthrough came with Medicare: a fully federal insurance program for those over 65 covering 80 percent of expenses, and Medicaid, a means-tested program to insure the low-income and shared with the states. Johnson brought Truman to his bill signing ceremony, and a major step toward universal health care seemed certain, but fate ran the effort off the rails. Although Nixon toyed with some ideas of

---

[70] In 1942, Sir William Beveridge issued the report *Social Insurance and Allied Services* calling for national health care. After winning a parliamentary majority in July 1945, the Labour government of Clement Atlee constructed the framework of the National Health Service in 1946 which remains the health care platform of Britain today.

Insidious Changes

universal coverage, these languished, and the fallout of Watergate greatly damaged the image of Washington politicians. Finally, the Reagan Revolution solidified the villainy of big government, and universal health care under the auspice of the federal government became a distant goal, but the idea did not die.

Bill Clinton campaigned heavily on universal health care. One of his first moves put his wife Hillary in charge of a task force to develop a program. After a year of closed meetings, Hillary's work rolled out to heavy criticism, including the American Medical Association and health insurance companies. Hillarycare became a term of derision.

The Clinton plan would require insurance and provide subsidies for coverage. Large employers were required to foot much of the cost, and the federal government would provide revenue to the states for implementing and maintaining the system. Abortion and pre-existing conditions would be covered in the program, and health management organizations (HMOs) became the vehicle of health care delivery. Also, a National Health Board would be established to oversee the operation of the program. The opposition mounted with the "Harry and Louise" commercials proving to be especially effective, and in the end, Clinton's Health Security Act failed. In the aftermath, Congress turned over to the Republicans in the 1994 election. Again, health care languished on the sidelines, but again, the idea and political will did not die. Along with senators Ted Kennedy and Orin Hatch, the Clinton administration passed the State Children Insurance Program (SCHIP, administered by the states) in 1997, providing means-tested insurance assistance for families with children. With SCHIP in place, it would be over a decade before the effort for universal coverage revived in a meaningful manner.

During the summer of 2009, President Obama and House Speaker Nancy Pelosi unveiled their 1,000-page solution for national health care. The bill would eventually morph into over 2,700 pages, and Pelosi would make the famous statement claiming that the bill needed to be passed to know what was in it. The plan had almost all of the features of the Clinton plan. By a narrow, partisan margin, the bill passed, and Obama signed it into law in March 2010. Obamacare became the law of the land, but not without challenge.

Obamacare almost immediately went to federal court, and eventually to the Supreme Court. Here the Obama administration

~ 150 ~

argued one day that the program contained no taxes, only penalties, and the next day it argued that the program did include a tax. In the final decision of *National Federation of Independent Business v. Sebelius*, Chief Justice Roberts joined four liberal justices (Ruth Bader Ginsburg, Stephen Breyer, Sonia Sotomayor, and Elena Kagan) choosing the poison of taxes to uphold the overall constitutionality of the program while striking down the individual mandate. A minimum level of coverage, the chief justice wrote, could not be upheld through the commerce clause, designed to regulate commerce not force economic activity, but a mandated payment, although argued as both a penalty and a tax by the Obama administration, would be considered a tax falling under the tax and spending authority of Congress.[71] Additionally, Roberts included in his decision that states could not be forced into Medicaid expansion, nor could they be punished if they did not participate, i.e., base funds could not be reduced if states did not expand coverage. Further challenges with Obamacare acceptance continued.

President Obama repeatedly made the comments that people could keep their doctors and their health care plans if they chose to do so. Suspicious voters began to organize into what became known as Tea Parties and confronted Democrat Members of Congress when they returned to their districts for visits (no Republican voted for the bill). As a result, the Democrats lost control of the House of Representatives in 2010. However, their retention of the Senate and White House made the survival of Obamacare a certainty. Eventually, health care consumers began to pay more for insurance, found their doctors unavailable, and learned from Obamacare's main architect, Massachusetts Institute of Technology Professor Jonathon Gruber, that the health care advocates had indeed lied to help move the legislation through the process.[72] These developments fueled a

---

[71] Conservative justices Antonin Scalia, Clarence Thomas, Samuel Alito, joined by the more libertarian Anthony Kennedy in a strong dissent to note that the language of the bill referred to a penalty, therefore the Taxing and Spending Clause of Congress could not be applied. However, the majority would further underpin the tax argument in 2015 with the *King v. Burwell* decision.

[72] "'Obamacare' Expert Apologizes for Remarks on Law's Creation, National Public Radio, retrieved from https://www.npr.org/tags/363539406/jonathan-gruber ; also YouTube, retrieved from  https://www.youtube.com/watch?v=Adrdmmh7bMo .

rollback of Democrat-controlled state legislatures, governorships, and eventually the US House, Senate, and presidency. Although the Republican House had voted down Obamacare more than 50 times, they had no substitute plan when they had full control, and the thumbs down of Senator John McCain sealed the fate of Obamacare remaining as law. Eventually, however, the Republican Congress and president removed the funding mechanism of taxes (penalties) based on failing to have health insurance. In 2018, based on the funding repeal, a Texas circuit judge ruled Obamacare unconstitutional as it had been based on congressional authority to tax, which had been removed. The drama continues.

## THE IMPACT OF THE ROBERTS COURT

*Since the appointment of Earl Warren to the high bench, Republican presidents have been seeking judges who would be consistently conservative voices in the Supreme Court. This search has proven to be tricky, and the appointment of John Roberts has not been an exception. Although he seemed conservative in early decisions such as the 2nd Amendment question of the Heller case, his tortured consideration of the individual mandate, which became a proclaimed tax to preserve Obamacare, caused observers to question his orientation.*

With the death of Chief Justice William Rehnquist in 2005, President George W. Bush nominated John Roberts for the top position on the Supreme Court. The Roberts Court was originally viewed as conservative, but as noted above, the Obamacare decision of 2012 threw this evaluation into question. However, there have been some conservative decisions.

The *District of Columbia v. Heller* case of 2008 showed the conservative side of the Roberts Court. A long-standing dispute over the interpretation of the 2nd Amendment came to a showdown with the Heller case. The immediate question at hand concerned the restrictive gun laws of the District of Columbia. The 1975 ordinance banned all handgun ownership other than those owned prior to the enactment of the law, and for licensed law enforcement officials. Also, rifles and shotguns were to be kept unloaded, and disassembled or trigger

~ 152 ~

locked.  The case would be dismissed at the district level, but the District of Columbia Appellate Court revived the lawsuit.  The decision illustrates the two interpretations of the 2nd Amendment, but ultimately the Court gave the decision to the individual right to own guns.

The 1939 *US v. Miller* decision held that the 2nd Amendment allowed any state to provide for private gun ownership to support the state militia: "A well regulated Militia, being necessary to the security of a free State, the right of the people to keep and bear Arms, shall not be infringed."  In the appellate dissent, Judge Henderson argued that the District of Columbia, not being a state and therefore not encumbered by the 2nd Amendment, could place restrictive laws on gun owners.  However, the majority took the individual approach in its interpretation.

The majority opinion in the appellate decision argued that the 2nd Amendment refers to an individual right held before the writing of our current constitution in 1787.  In fact, individual gun ownership allowed militias to exist.  Finally, the court included handguns as arms as defined under the 2nd Amendment.

With the Supreme Court appeal, numerous *amicus curiae* petitions were filed, over twice as many urging the Court to uphold the appellate decision versus those seeking to overturn the ruling.  In the end, the Roberts Court upheld the individual right of ownership interpretation and included handguns in that interpretation.  The Court opined that gun ownership is not only a right for public protection, the militia, but also individual protection.  It finally concluded that these rights were established in American society before the adoption of the current constitution.

As much as conservatives applauded the Heller decision, the Obamacare ruling made them scratch their heads in question with the *Obergefell v. Hodges* decision, which legalized same-sex marriage in all states through the 14th Amendment.  Although Roberts held with the conservatives on Obergefell, allowing the states to determine laws concerning same-sex marriages, he veered off the conservative trail allowing the argument for Obamacare by determining that the individual mandate equated to a tax and fell under the right of taxation given to Congress in Article I, Section 8.

Supreme Court justices are a hard lot to predict.  Eisenhower did not expect the outcome the country received with Earl Warren on the

Insidious Changes

bench.  Some analysts believe Roberts himself has latent liberal tendencies, while others speculate that he is attempting to replace Anthony Kennedy as the moderate/swing vote on the Court.  Only time will tell.  However, one thing for certain, the political fight will continue.

## IMPEACHMENT: TODAY'S POLITICAL WEAPON OF CHOICE?

*Rarely considered in the past, the Congressional tool of impeachment has been used three times in the last half-century against presidents. This usage seems to be an outgrowth of the political tension that has overtaken the US since the late 1960s and early 1970s.  The tool to be used if presidents (or other public officials) became corrupted or criminal seems to be edging further towards Alexander Hamilton's fear that it would transform into nothing more than a political weapon for those seeking power.*

The Constitution is based on structured struggle and conflict.  The separation of powers and checks and balances ensure that tension will always exist between the federal branches.  Although somewhat muted over time, the 10th amendment reserving power to the states adds to the tension.  However, since Vietnam and Watergate, politics has steadily increased the tension of governing, reaching new heights during the past few years.

Alexander Hamilton had inhibitions concerning the mechanism of impeachment, believing that the legislature would encroach on judiciary authority and that it could devolve into political battles aligning political opponents against each other.  Although he expressed his doubts in the *Federalist Papers*, he eventually decided that the system would be imperfect, but could be managed.  For years he would be proven correct, but if he returned today, he might well decide that his first reaction was correct.

Congress would threaten John Adams with censure (not listed in the Constitution) over the extradition of Thomas Nash, a British mutineer who took refuge in Charleston, SC.  The Senate did issue a censure against Andrew Jackson for his dealings with the Bank of the United States but expunged it a few years later.  Articles of

~ 154 ~

Impeachment were actually drawn up against John Tyler for his use of the veto, but the effort died before being heard in committee. After the Civil War, Andrew Johnson became the first president impeached for violation of the Tenure in Office statute (the Senate had to agree to remove an approved political appointee). The effort to remove Johnson eventually failed in the Senate by one vote. The "nuclear option," if you will, of removal from office took a breather for many years, but came back with a vengeance in the last half of the 20th Century.

Friction grew between Congress and Richard Nixon, eventually hitting a breaking point with Watergate. Independent counsel, congressional committees, and news investigations persisted for months, even years. This friction reached a boiling point with the Saturday Night Massacre (see Being Borked section above), but the president held his line. Finally, when Nixon lost his battle to maintain the secrecy of his Oval Office tapes, the impeachment possibility became more of a real possibility. Rather than face almost certain removal from office, Nixon resigned only to be pardoned by his successor Gerald Ford. Two decades later, the continual scandals surrounding the Clinton administration dominated headlines. Again, independent investigations led the way over a bevy of questionable issues from the Clintons' investment in the White Water development in Arkansas to the firing of the White House travel staff when Bill reached the presidency. However, all of this fell short of impeachment until the revelation of Bill's affair with Monica Lewinsky, a White House intern. Eventually, the impeachment process failed in the Senate, and Clinton completed his term (Bill would lose his license to practice law over the perjury charge). Congress had a dicey relationship with George W. Bush and Barack Obama's administration, but no censure or impeachment articles came forward. However, this would change with the 45th president.

Almost immediately upon the election of Donald Trump as president, some of his political opponents began calling for his removal through impeachment. For two years, a special investigation with Robert Mueller at the helm drug on and on, resulting in some of Trump's close advisors being placed in prison. However, when Mueller submitted the final report, no smoking gun of "High crimes and misdemeanors" would be found. Not to be deterred, the Democrat House turned and immediately started moving in another

~ 155 ~

direction, this time concerning relations with Ukraine, seeking articles to remove the president. Even states have gotten into the act with California passing a statute attempting to make Trump reveal his financial history or be barred from the state primary. As this book goes to print, the Democrat House failed in its slow-moving impeachment process but is threatening other impeachment filings against the chief executive. Also, there have been Democrat discussions of impeaching newly appointed Justice Brett Kavanaugh, seen as the possible vote to overturn the Roe decision. Obviously, and unfortunately, Hamilton's concerns might be coming true.

# X. COMMENTS ON CURRENT POLITICAL TENSIONS

*"If we can but prevent the government from wasting the labours of the people, under the pretence of taking care of them, they must become happy." ~ Thomas Jefferson*

Safety is an elusive state for humanity. We seek it, but rarely is it found. Oh sure, if we make the right career moves, save with the proven methods, and are not subject to a hostile company takeover and "reorganization," we might gain some level of safety and security. However, most of us know people who seem to have it all but then are cut down in a car accident or fall victim to cancer or some other malady. There really is no guarantee in life, but our inherent longing for safety and security drives us to continually search for it, no matter how elusive or unrealistic the quest. This inherent longing keeps socialism relevant in our minds despite the fact that its historical reality has been the opposite of unity and abundance. Contrary to the empirical record from the former Soviet Union, North Korea, China, Cuba, or the recent Venezuelan disaster, the utopian call of socialism persists and serves as a simple answer to the challenges of this life while in reality causing tension and disappointment.

The political divisions that emerged after the shattering of the New Deal Coalition in 1968 have only deepened over the years. The shootings at Kent State, the revelation of CIA activities, turmoil in Vietnam, and the Nixon White House continually churned the waters. The complexion of Washington politics reflected the new fracturing immediately after Watergate as House subcommittees exploded, and seniority decreased in value. In the Congress that convened in January 1975, legislators expected to be heard and relevant in the governing halls on Capitol Hill. Everyone wanted input, and that mentality has only increased over the years as old structures of seniority fell apart.

Technology has only increased the emphasis on the individual politician. A recent prime example is Alexandria Ocasio-Cortez (AOC) from New York City. How does a representative buried in a

Insidious Changes

borough of the Big Apple become a household name? Twitter, Facebook, and other forms of social media translate into TV coverage. Exposure is the key! Oh, and the more outrageous your demands, well, the more you just fit in with popular culture. As silly as all this might seem when written on paper, it works. Let's take a look at two extremes.

On the left, AOC refers to herself as a democratic socialist and endorsed Bernie Sanders for president, who also proclaims to be a democratic socialist while running for the nomination of the Democrat Party. What is a democratic socialist? Well, they are socialists, and that leads to some principles that are at odds with the American experience.

The platform of the Democratic Socialist Party of the USA states that:

> Democratic socialists believe that both the economy
> and society should be run democratically—to meet
> public needs, not to make profits for a few. To achieve
> a more just society, many structures of our government
> and economy must be radically transformed through
> greater economic and social democracy so that
> ordinary Americans can participate in the many
> decisions that affect our lives.[73]

In other words, the collective is primary to the individual. The individual will not reap the benefits of his/her efforts; instead the needs of all will be part of the process to distribute goods and services. This is similar to the platform of the Socialist Party of the USA. It reads:

> The Socialist Party stands for the abolition of every
> form of domination and exploitation . . . .
> We are committed to the transformation of capitalism
> through the creation of a socialist society . . . Socialism
> will establish a new social and economic order in
> which workers and community members will take
> responsibility for and control of their interpersonal
> relationships, their neighborhoods, the local

---

[73] About US, Democratic Socialist Party of the USA, retrieved from https://www.dsausa.org/about-us/ .

~ 158 ~

Insidious Changes

government, and the production and distribution of all goods and services.

For these reasons, we call for social ownership and democratic control of productive resources, for a guarantee to all of the right to participate in societal production, and to a fair share of society's product, in accordance with individual needs.[74]

The Communist Party of the USA, still paying homage to Marx and his theory of revolutionary history, panders a softer line mimicking the other socialist parties. Their website reads they are working for, ". . . a brighter future, one based on democracy, peace, justice, equality, cooperation, and meeting human needs. That future is socialism, a system in which working people control their own lives and destinies, and together build a better world."[75] Control and justice, it sounds so simple! However, the truth is much different.

Sweden tried socialism and backed off. China, North Korea, Cuba, Venezuela, the old Soviet Union, as well as other countries proclaiming socialism, have been a trail of disaster and human waste. The "better world" never developed. Estimates vary, but it is generally agreed that tens of millions of people have died because of socialism/communism. The murderous regimes far outpace Adolf Hitler (national socialism) in killing efficiency, confiscated property, and imprisonment without any semblance of due process. Despite all this reality, young Americans are hearing the siren call of socialism and responding with 65 percent of those under 30 voting for Sanders in the 2020 Nevada state primary.[76] This may seem odd to those who are older, but it is not all that puzzling.

When we are young, we seek answers. Toddlers go through the "why?" phase, but this is more than just a phase. We continue to search for answers in our lives, but we pursue this through different means: reading, seeking out experiences, etc. The young adults still seeking answers become young voters seeking answers as well as

---

[74] Platform, Socialist Party of the USA, retrieved from https://www.socialistpartyusa.net/platform.

[75] Program, Communist Party of the USA, retrieved from https://www.cpusa.org/party_info/party-program/.

[76] "Here's Why Kids These Days Love Socialism," CNN, retrieved from https://www.youtube.com/watch?v=kxb4kN06XGk.

Insidious Changes

solutions. Why is the world so unfair? Can I make a difference? Yes, the socialist will take control and right the wrongs! However, there are a significant number of young voters rejecting control and seek answers within, the opposite of the socialist solution. These voters are commonly referred to as libertarians.

The Libertarian Party came into existence in 1971 and steadily gained enough electoral success to become a third party fixture in US elections. However, they could not win elections as Libertarians in our winner-take-all system (whoever gets the most votes wins the seat). So, what did they do? They formed the Republican Liberty Caucus, often passing themselves off as conservatives. Their website reads:

- We seek to substantially reduce the size and intrusiveness of government and cut and eliminate taxes at every opportunity.
- We believe that peaceful, honest people should be able to offer their goods and services to willing consumers without inappropriate interference from government.
- We believe that peaceful, honest people should decide for themselves how to live their lives, without fear of criminal or civil penalties.
- We believe that government's only responsibility, if any, should be protecting people from force and fraud.[77]

It is easy to see why they fit in more with the conservative Republicans than the modern liberal Democrats, and not being able to win on their own, they caucus with a major party. Smart politics! However, there are some sticking points. Being conservative, the more traditional Republicans take exception with legalized marijuana, while Libertarians believe its consumption should be an individual choice. Abortion is also a sticking point as Republicans tend to be pro-life, and the Libertarian Party considers it within the realm of the individual not to be touched by government. Finally, Republicans tend to be strong on foreign policy (the very core of a Reagan Republican), and Libertarians tend to be much more isolationist. Rand Paul often speaks on TV as a Republican, but the fact is he follows in his father's, Ron Paul's, footsteps of libertarianism.

---

[77] About Us, Libertarian Party, retrieved from https://www.lp.org/about/.

Insidious Changes

The libertarian is not all that hard for conservatives to accept. Libertarians believe in free markets, limited government, and individualism, all essential elements of the Reagan Republican. Sure, they are a little liberal on social issues, but this can be handled, the scales fall in favor of the alignment. However, this is not the case with liberal Democrats and socialists; there are some significant differences.

Modern liberals sharply divide with socialists on a minimum of three issues: socialist are radical, they do not believe in the Constitution or American institutions, and although tried in many countries over many decades, socialism has never worked. "You are being a little dramatic, aren't you?" you might ask. No, not really. Let me explain.

Economies can be placed on a continuum of total, centralized control by the government, and at the other end, a fully free market economy. Total control came closest to being a reality in the old Soviet Union, while the post Civil War period of the American 19th Century will work as the closest model here. So, the continuum would appear something like this:

| Types of Economies | |
| --- | --- |
| Command | Free Market |
| Old Soviet Union | 19th Century US |

Markets go up, and markets go down. This keeps the economy dynamic and responsive to the consumer. If personal computer technology enters the marketplace, typewriters will become a thing of the past. This example can be repeated several times over history, horse buggies replaced by cars, reciprocal piston engines replaced by jet engines, etc. All these product changes resulted from some product falling in favor with the consumer, and the new rising in favor. This might be a failure in some minds, but economic progress in others.

It might be difficult to understand failure as success. Taking a look back at inventors in history, we find that they tried, and usually tried again, and again, and probably several times before having success. It is the numerous failures that teach lessons and moves us forward to final success. Ask those who tinker in the machine shops around the country, and you will find the same pattern. The problem

~ 161 ~

with socialism is it promises to replace risk with everything a person needs, everything but one essential element, incentive.

The allure of socialism is that it promises our basic needs will be met. However, there is no incentive to produce these goods. There is no reward for making a better product and seeing it flourish in the marketplace. No thrill of making life better by developing a labor-saving device. Life becomes mere existence, a grinding existence: show up, work, you may get enough to feed yourself, but you will never have enough to feel comfortable or gain a feeling of individual accomplishment. With that in mind, let's expand our continuum a bit.

The Americans I run into who call for socialism (this is usually young people) fail to realize they are really seeking more safety net, that inherent search for security. They desire more of the welfare state, more of the Western European welfare state, not really socialism with all its disincentives. There are two problems with this scenario: one is the amount of taxes paid to support the welfare state, and two, the Western European countries are much more centralized than the US system. Here is a quick comparison of some of the welfare states:

| Types of Economies | | |
|---|---|---|
| Command | Welfare State | Free Market |
| Old USSR | France/Finland/Belgium/Denmark/Italy/UK/ US (since the New Deal) | US (19th Century) |

Of those countries listed, the US is the least active of the welfare states, while France has the most invested in the state-run system. Take another look at the chart and guess which countries have the highest taxes. You would be correct if you move to the left of the welfare block (they will fall in slightly different order, but they are the same countries). Why are the taxes so high in welfare states? Because it is a form of redistribution (akin to socialism), and the taxes remove cash from the high earners to the lower end of the wage scale. This can be done a bit more efficiently in a smaller, more centralized country than a federal system like the US, which has multiple spheres of governmental jurisdiction.

When approached with the idea of having more welfare programs in the US, I respond with a question. I like using questions because it tends to keep the personal aspect to a minimum in the debate and

Insidious Changes

focuses on issues that are known by most intelligent people. I usually begin with the preface that our goal is to deliver aid programs to those who need assistance. "So, how we can be more efficient?" is the first question I pose. I believe that one way is to have block grants and let the states follow some simple guidelines for distribution (the Trump administration favored this method for COVID-19 programs), which seems reasonable (those close to the problem should know the problem best). Keep the goods close to home for better oversight and efficient spending, I offer as additional support. However, those on the left of the political scale do not like this answer of decentralization as they seem to prefer bigger programs translating into more spending. So, my second question is, "Do you believe that Americans will support more taxes?" Sometimes I am answered with, "I would be willing to pay more taxes," and I must clarify the question. I am not asking if you would pay more, I mean Americans as a whole. The response, once the question gets past the personal resistance, usually ends the discussion. Of course, the answer for many Americans is that they do not mind taxes going up on those with higher incomes, but when it comes to their pocketbook, forget it!

So, in light of the evidence and logic, why is socialism growing in favor among younger Americans? I believe there are two basic reasons: one, it is a simple solution, and two, the young tend to view the American system negatively. As mentioned before, young people are inclined to ask why? Why do people suffer in the richest country in the world? Why do some have more money than they can ever spend while others do not have enough to survive? Add to this the anti-American bias in many social science and humanities departments of universities around the country, and an alternative path seems to be the only answer to the tragedies of our country. Again, a simple solution is very inviting to those with little experience. Of course, the point of this book is to provide a door to our historical experience and provide an alternative point of view.

Insidious Changes

# XI. QUESTIONS AND ANSWERS

*"Only a virtuous people are capable of freedom. As nations become corrupt and vicious, they have more need of masters."*
~ Benjamin Franklin

"That is all well and fine," you might say to me, "but what should we do about it?" That is a very fair question for any policymaker who outlines a problem. In fact, I expect answers from those who outline public policy problems to me. Therefore, this section will explore some approaches you, me, and every American can employ to improve our quality of life and ensure the freedom of self-government for years to come. I'll begin by relating some of my personal story.

I have stood on the floor of the Missouri House of Representatives for the last eight years watching my fellow legislators talk past each other, and I mean *knowingly* talk past each other! It is truly amazing how two groups of people, supposedly devoted to the same framework of government, can disagree on practically everything they have presented to them. However, during this time I came to the realization that the two sides lived in polar opposite universes, one believing the Constitution to be a document of ground rules for limited government and preservation of individual rights while the other believed it had evolved into a different, more active governmental structure with some (I mean limited) basic tenets of individual liberty. These two trains had been heading toward each other for quite a while, but today they are head-to-head, and neither seems to be backing off.

To illustrate the changes of the last century, we can use the centennial of the 19th Amendment. With the amendment, the activists took the route of changing the Constitution. They first made changes at the state level, and eventually found the support to change the Constitution in the manner provided by the Founders (amendment ratification through three-fourths of the state legislatures). On the other hand, we have the examples of Roe and Obergefell: unelected officials cramming their interpretation of societal well-being into statutes and constitutional context that impact all of the electorate despite their state constitutions and statutes. Same-sex marriage is a

~ 165 ~

prime example of the minority of black robes in opposition to the vast majority of the electorate. After 28 states affirmed their interpretation of marriage in the traditional manner, the US Supreme Court joined several other state judges and rejected the social interpretation of the voters. The problem here is the appearance of being arbitrary and elitist. It is easy to justify many actions in the mind, but how will these thoughts play out in the real world? We could move through a long list of government policies running headlong into reality: Prohibition, various welfare programs, and busing, just to name a few.[78] Add to this the appearance of elites overturning the vote of the people and the perception of being ruled rather than ruling can easily increase for the average American.

One foundational principle of self-government is debate, an exercise designed to provide examples and concerns of many different communities before any policy or policy change is enacted. In the legislature, this is a drawn-out process that requires weeks, months, even years to complete and includes a wide variety of people. This process is in stark contrast to a bench trial (an appeal is a review of the facts by jurists, not a jury) that typically takes a few hours to argue, a few people directly affected by the outcome testify, and a handful of government officials make the final decision. However, every American should keep in mind that public policy is a two-edged sword: we may get what we want taking the short cut of the courts, but there will be long-term societal effects! Over the years, I have encountered several issues of policy that need to be considered in a broad context.

I served my community in the statehouse constantly inundated by proposals that made sense, were self-serving, and the vast majority that required thought and consideration of other perspectives. My observation from that experience is that narrow-minds, and narrow special interests, produce bad legislation. However, there is also

---

[78] Even a cursory review of the time period for busing reveals that the policy may have helped integrate schools, but it begs the question: at what social cost? Neither blacks nor whites relished the idea of placing their kids on buses for several more hours a week to attend a school in a distant neighborhood. The Washington Post had a good review of the polling and history of busing on 7 July 2019, retrieved from https://www.washingtonpost.com/national/effective-but-never-popular-court-ordered-busing-is-a-relic-few-would-revive/2019/07/07/dce439c8-9d40-11e9-b27f-ed2942f73d70_story.html .

Insidious Changes

another side to the process. A mind that turns inward and rationalizes from a theoretical perspective only invites division, conflict, and yes, even electoral ramifications. In fly-over country where I live, we believe that policy must be peppered with a fair dose of common sense, or the "Will it work in the real world?" test. Frankly, this should be asked by a policymaker numerous times throughout the debate process. This should also be modified by another truism; the government is not the end-all-be-all that rectifies every problem in the world.

As this book reached completion, the Coronavirus (COVID-19) outbreak hit. The power of the centralized state came to full force. President Trump declared emergency executive powers, Congress started promising checks in the mail, and the Federal Reserve started slashing interest rates. Now, don't get me wrong, the world has changed, and government must change or become irrelevant. My issue is how the change occurred. I don't expect perfect; there never will be such in this world. However, we could make an attempt to stay with the original format and make it comply with our current needs. National emergencies give the executive enormous powers, rightly so, but these should be temporary and tailored to fit the need.

It seems very attractive to lean on the promises of FDR in his Four Freedoms Speech, and the COVID-19 situation energized the modern liberals to transform our government into a more "progressive" form (i.e., central control). However, a question must be asked concerning this blanket of comfort offered by the federal government and its bevy of experts: at what price? Freedom from want, is that possible? What might we spend trying to reach the impossible? The first rule we learn in economics is that of scarcity: unlimited wants coupled with limited resources. Governments provide the environment to prosper, not prosperity itself. When is the last time you had a really good experience with a government agency? I mean, walking away without paying money, moving through at an efficient pace, a belief that your best interests were in the minds of every worker, and they happened to be focused on the quality of service and efficiency? If you've had all of these happen to you lately, I think you had a very unusual experience.[79]

---

[79] The Trump administration frustrated the Democrats with cooperative federalism. Trump met the COVID-19 crisis head on initially by taking executive

Insidious Changes

Governments tend to be slow and cumbersome. The recent COVID-19 situation demonstrated that we do indeed have a government safety net, not a government-provides-all system. Unemployment claims quickly overwhelmed the state agencies designed to provide these services. Small businesses came in droves to claim federal loans that could become grants if used for payroll and found the typical government queue: hurry up and wait! What if this became the norm? You only need to ask our southern neighbors in Cuba or Venezuela for the answer.

All goods and services are doled out in some manner. In a market economy, that placement is achieved through price: those willing to part with the money receive the goods and services. Those with more money have more choices, and those with less have fewer, but in a healthy, functioning market economy, these fewer choices will be adequate: maybe not steak every night, but certainly protein of some type. If the goods are not available, there is a problem, most likely with government. In a market economy, the goods will find the consumer. If the consumer cannot work, has no family, and no other resources in his/her community, the government must step in to fill the void. However, it is best for the government to keep the market working. If that is accomplished, then consumer needs will be met. If the government over-regulates, bans certain items from the market or entices populations into unsustainable environments (inadequate water supply, for example), then the consumer suffers.

I think we all agree that medicine must have some level of regulation. Medicines should be pure. We should receive the amounts we pay for, *sans* the thumb on the scale! Those giving medical advice should be qualified. However, what price level is correct for this assurance? The medical profession has become the epitome of regulatory capture in an industry.

---

action. Shutting down travel from affected areas proved to be a critical first step. Next, the Federal Reserve cranked its economic policy mechanism into action. However, he did not attempt to direct every move from his podium. Instead, he sought ways to assist the states with provisions of supplies, FEMA support where needed, providing guidelines to be shaped by governors and states on a case-by-case basis. Just as New York is different from California which is different from Missouri, Trump gave guidelines and allowed the governments closer to the people to serve the people.

Insidious Changes

Most of us are not medical professionals.  We might (and should) know some basics, but nowhere near the level of an expert.  For this quality of information, we seek out medical doctors, and we expect these doctors to be qualified.  Therefore, the state should license these professional experts.  These experts can provide a great deal of knowledge to legislators and regulators, but they are also in business.  Those in business are generally there to make money.  So, the question becomes, how much advice from the American Medical Association is best for the patients, and how much is in the interest of the profession/business?

I could have used several different industries to illustrate my point, but I chose medicine because it is such a part of the public debate.  We all need health care at some point.  Modern medicine has made great strides and continues to improve in many aspects of treatment and cure.  However, are we going to continue to offer everyone access at a high price, or will we let the high prices develop these cures and treatments, and then let mass production sustain the business after development?  Everyone cannot have everything.  However, with the market system, everyone can have more.

These thoughts take me back to 1984 when conservative icon William F. Buckley, Jr. visited my local public institution of higher education, the University of Central Missouri (Central Missouri State University at the time).[80]  During Buckley's remarks, he commented that liberalism offers no final solutions.  Knowing the man as a devout Catholic, I believe his remark referred to the imperfect world we live in and the fact that it will continue to be imperfect as long as humans are involved.  Humans will always fall short of perfect, but Christians believe much of what we do as individuals can make a difference.[81]

---

[80] Buckley launched his public life with a critique of the liberal curriculum in higher education with his 1951 bestseller *God and Man at Yale*.  He solidified the late 20th Century conservative movement with the publication of the periodical *National Review* in 1955.  An early supporter of Joseph McCarthy, Buckley later filtered out what he believed to be fringe groups such as the John Birch Society, Ayn Rand and her followers, and supported civil rights expansion although initially hesitant about federal action.  His television show "Firing Line" ran for 33 years and his syndicated newspaper column "On the Right" ran in over 300 publications at its peak.  *National Review* is still in publication despite Buckley's death in 2008.

[81] Jesus advised his followers to be kind to the poorest in the world, those who can really do nothing in return for you.  In other words, be kind to others, we are all in this together!  Matthew 25: 40-45.

The liberalism offered by human thinkers cannot possibly deliver all things to all people, this is impossible, so don't expect everything the Feds offer. This is my first and maybe most important piece of advice and leads me to another recommendation.

My second piece of advice is bet more on people you know than people you don't know. The old saying goes that "familiarity breeds contempt," but those you see every day could be the best leaders for your community. They struggle with the same issues you encounter, things from poverty to addiction. Those in Washington, DC, have proven time and again their policies become cumbersome and are partially effective while a strong economy certainly cures issues such as poverty.[82] Sure, if you donate tens of thousands at a time to one of the national committees or a federal candidate's political action committee (PAC), maybe you can bet on people you don't know, but you always need to ask yourself, does this person know my community? If not, the next question is, can this person relate to my community through some life experience they have had? If you are the average donor and cannot answer either of these in the affirmative, it might be wise to keep the bulk of your money closer to home. Let me illustrate.

There is an often-told story of an old man meeting a young girl on the beach one morning. The girl is picking up starfish and throwing them back into the water after high tide. "What are you doing?" the old man asked. "I'm putting these starfish back into the ocean," the little girl replies. The old man put out his arms and swung them back and forth. "Look at all these starfish," he said, "there must be thousands. You can't possibly believe you can make a difference with so many starfish in need," he said in a forlorn voice. Undeterred, the young girl picked up another starfish and flung it as far as she could back into the ocean. "I made a difference to that one," she answered and moved on down the beach continuing her mission. From the mouths of babes! Again, a policy question to ask is, will this candidate enhance or hinder the efforts within my state and my community that strive to make a better place of my little piece of the world? Is the candidate willing to let you and your community

---

[82] US Department of Health and Human Services, "Poverty in the United States: 50-Year Trends and Safety Net Impacts," retrieved from, https://aspe.hhs.gov/system/files/pdf/154286/50YearTrends.pdf .

Insidious Changes

function, or seeking to perpetuate a system of top-down control? If you like your answer, support the candidate, if not, seek another.

Self-government is not limited to government. It is part of civil society, a society filled with people that respect and care for each other. This does not mean that I am always right, that my way is all or it is the highway for you! It means that I give people the space to live their lives without controlling their every move. It also means that I need not accept, or publicly celebrate, every move and action of every other person. It means, be kind, wish them a nice day, don't worry about your neighbor's business unless asked. There is an old country saying, "Good fences make good neighbors." There is another saying that is religious by nature, but certainly a good guide for every person: Do unto others as you would have them do unto you. Almost every religion has some form of the Golden Rule, so it is certainly self-defeating to say there should be a complete and total separation of religion from the state. If government is all about people, the least government can do is allow others to teach us how to be civil to other people. Bet more on people than government: this is a principle of our founding, and certainly something our Founders understood.

The Founders were so effective because they were philosophical, practical, and understood the world and human nature to the extent of building safeguards into their framework of self-government. They also knew three fundamental issues would be critical to the survival of the Union:

1. There must be some uniform set of rules if we are all to prosper. They set about to establish a community of commerce, what we would label a national economy, to facilitate exchange, and allow all to prosper.
2. Enemies are out there, and they must be dealt with in an effective manner. This they called the common defense.
3. Finally, if people are free, they can achieve amazing things with their creativity and ingenuity. These principles are grounded in our Constitution and protected in a variety of ways, including the Bill of Rights.[83] They knew multiple

---

[83] The Founders were quite concerned about self-government and the behavior of people. Knowing that they could not control the behavior, they appealed to civility ensured by religion. The Virginia Declaration of Rights, serving as the model for

Insidious Changes

safeguards would be needed to preserve what generations of resourceful enemies would attempt to destroy.

Remember, it's all about people. We are all Americans. We proclaim principles to the world that better the condition of people. This has been the history and mission of the country since its founding. It took many years for the tent of opportunity to expand, but it did because those visionary leaders of Colonial America understood a virtuous republic could prosper if we remain true to the principles that serve all.

One final note on people: do not scuttle relationships over politics. I am certain there are many things American liberals and American conservatives can agree on, and the disagreements should not poison the well of community. Unfortunately, no system is one hundred percent failsafe, and believe it or not, I have lost friends over policy differences. Some of these have been longtime friends! They don't always say they are upset with me, but I can tell, their attitude shines through in their mannerisms, all the while avoiding words. I feel for them in a way, but I know I can't change them, and until I receive better information, I must go with what I have evaluated as correct. So, I vote as I vote, and the citizens decide to retain or replace me: this philosophy served me well until I reached the term limits of the Missouri Constitution.

The bottom line assessment is that the Founders created a system of personal liberty that allows for political and economic freedom. The two cannot be separated, and this fact has played out over several centuries. Political influence sprouts from having the ability to support one's life, family, and finally, community. Repressive governments throughout history have denied the fundamental economic freedom to flourish and held onto power through citizen dependence. Is that really what the future of the US should be? Is that really prosperity and progress? Can any human reach his/her full potential if they are dependent on government for basic necessities?

At the beginning of this book, I asked if you would purposely put diesel in your gasoline engine? I answered I hope not because you

---

the Bill of Rights, included the comment in Article 16, ". . . all men are equally entitled to the free exercise of religion, according to the dictates of conscience, and that it is the mutual duty of all to practise Christian forbearance, love, and charity toward each other.", retrieved from, https://www.archives.gov/founding-docs/virginia-declaration-of-rights.

Insidious Changes

know the outcome would not be good if you did take such action. Of course, you would have the same outcome whether you knowingly or unknowingly put the wrong fuel in your vehicle. Eventually, the engine would be ruined. Unfortunately, this metaphor is very relevant to our constitutional government today: knowingly and unknowingly, Americans are damaging the institutions of self-government that have served us well for more than two centuries. I ask that you take a look at your expectations for government, and in turn, what you are using as fuel to achieve your goals. What are you asking of government? Are you treating others around you as if they matter? Do you belong to a church and/or other benevolent association that asks you to donate time and money that ultimately benefits others? Or do you complain that the government does not do enough, vote for those politicians who promise the moon, and consider your conscience clear? Do you really understand federalism and keeping government close to the people it serves? Do you understand this connection of federalism to freedom, support it, and work to keep government as close to the people as possible? Or do you complain about the president because he's on the TV news every night and there are still problems in the world? Or do you make an effort to be informed and educated so that you understand and can distinguish between short-term goals and long-term benefits? The future of self-government in the US, that light upon the hill, depends on your answers.

Insidious Changes

# XII. A TIMELINE OF THE CONSTITUTION AND AMERICAN POLITICS

The following is a chronological listing of some of the most important dates in the history of the Constitution and American politics. This is intended as a guide to assist the reader in maintaining the historical order of these events.

## THE AMERICAN COLONIAL PERIOD

1492: Christopher Columbus landed in the Caribbean, the event that unleashed European colonization in the Americas.

1607: Captain Christopher Newport founded the first permanent English colony in America called Jamestown located in Virginia. Henry Hudson searched for a northern passage to the Pacific Ocean.

1611: An authorized English version of the Bible, the King James Version, published.

1612: Tobacco plantations were established in Virginia. The revenue from the crop solidified the colony's economy.

1614: Pocahontas converted to Christianity and married the Englishman John Rolfe; peace between Jamestown settlers and locals followed.

1619: The first representative assembly in America met at Jamestown. The first Africans were imported into Virginia, eventually becoming enslaved.

1620: A group of Puritans (religious dissenters seeking to "purify" the Anglican Church) left England on the "Mayflower" and landed on Cape Cod where they founded the Plymouth Plantation. Rough seas apparently resulted in the altering of the landing from Nantucket to an area outside the jurisdiction of Virginia. The non-Puritans were not

~ 175 ~

pleased and the two groups agreed to settle their differences with the "Mayflower Compact," a fundamental step in the American tradition of majority rule.

1626: The Dutch exchanged trinkets to Indians for the purchase of Manhattan Island, and there they established New Amsterdam.

1630: Boston was founded in the Great Migration of Puritans from England.

1632: Lord Baltimore was granted a charter to found the colony of Maryland.

1636: Harvard became the first established college in North America. After being banished from the Massachusetts Bay Colony, Roger Williams founded Providence Plantation.

1639: "The "Fundamental Orders" of Hartford, Wethersfield, and Windsor became the first written constitution in North America.

1641: Parliament abolished the Star Chamber and High Commission (formed under Elizabeth I), passed Puritan measures for the church, issued the "Grand Remonstrance" which listed its grievances against Charles I, and executed the earl of Stafford, a chief advisor of the king.

1642: The First (Great) English Civil War began when after Charles I attempted to arrest five Parliamentary members.

1643: The New England Confederation (also known as the United Colonies of New England) was formed to defend the colonies against the local tribes and New Netherland colonists. It would function at various levels until the 1680s.
At the age of four, Louis XIV became the king of France. He would remain on the throne until 1715, the longest reign of any European monarch.

Insidious Changes

1644: Parliamentary leader Oliver Cromwell soundly defeated the Royalists at Marston Moor, the deciding battle of Charles I's struggle with Parliament.

1645: The newly reorganized Parliamentary forces, the New Model Army, soundly defeated the Royalists at Naseby.

1646: Charles' Royalists forces were defeated at Oxford. Charles escaped to Scotland and surrendered to its Parliament which ended the First English Civil War.

1647: The Scots returned Charles to the English Parliament for a monetary payment. The Scots secretly planned to restore Charles to full power.

1648: The Second English Civil War began with Scotland's invasion into England, but the northerners lost to Cromwell. In Pride's Purge (conducted by Colonel Thomas Pride), the army dismissed all Presbyterians from Parliament citing them as Royalists and resulting in the "Rump Parliament" which ruled as a unicameral body. Parliament then agreed to try the king for treason.

1649: Maryland adopted the Toleration Act which allowed freedom of worship. In England, Charles I was found guilty of being a murderer, public enemy, tyrant, and traitor, and was executed. Oliver Cromwell and the army controlled the newly formed Commonwealth of England, and ruled through the Parliament. Scotland proclaimed Charles II as king.

1650: Cromwell defeated Scottish rebellions.

1651: Prince Charles, the King Charles I's son, fled to France. Thomas Hobbes published *Leviathan* which supported the king's absolute rule as derived from the consent of the ruled. The first

Insidious Changes

English Navigation Act restricted the shipment of goods from English colonies to England and on English ships.

1653: Parliament proclaimed Cromwell Lord Protector of the Commonwealth of England, Scotland, and Ireland under the Instrument of Government.

1655: The Dutch West India Company took control of New Sweden (present-day Delaware). A Royalist uprising failed: Cromwell dismissed Parliament and instituted martial law throughout England.

1656: War erupted between England and Spain. Cromwell recalled Parliament.

1657: Parliament replaced the Instrument of Government with the Humble Petition and Advice which reestablished a two house legislature (Cromwell nominated the upper house). France allied with England against the Spanish.

1658: Oliver Cromwell died and his son Richard succeeded to the leadership of England.

1659: Maryland declared its allegiance to Charles II. Richard Cromwell dissolved theis Parliament and the army reconvened the "Rump Parliament." The army eventually forced the resignation of Richard Cromwell, and George Monk raised a force in support of civilian government.

1660: George Monk occupied London and recalled the "Long Parliament" which dissolved itself in favor of a "Convention Parliament." Charles II issued the Declaration of Breda which promised amnesty and tolerance. He was soon restored to the throne by Parliament. New Navigation Act restricted North American colonial trade with nations other than England.

Insidious Changes

1663: French finance minister Jean Baptiste Colbert shaped New France into the province of Quebec. Charles II granted charters to the Royal African Company and the proprietors of North Carolina and Rhode Island.

1664: With the surrender of Peter Stuyvesant, England took possession of Dutch holdings in North America and renamed New Amsterdam to New York (Fort Orange became Albany).

1666: The Dutch and French declared war on England.

1669: Carolina established John Locke's constitution as its governing document.

1670: The Hudson's Bay Company became the chartered trading entity for the portion of North America that drained into the bay.

1674: The Treaty of Westminster gave English citizenship to the inhabitants of New Sweden and New York.

1675: King Phillip's War (Metacom's Rebellion) erupted in New England between the English settlers and their tribal allies against the Wampanoag and Narragansett tribes and their allies led by Metacom (known as Phillip).

1676: Bacon's rebellion erupted in Virginia when Nathaniel Bacon gained popular support with the issuance of the "Declaration of the People of Virginia." Roger Williams published a tract against Quakerism.

1677: Princess Mary, the daughter of the Duke of York, married William III of Orange.

1678: King Phillip's War (Metacom's Rebellion) ended with the Treaty of Casco Bay. Metacom was killed, about 1,000 colonists and 3,000 Indians died. Some New England towns were completely

Insidious Changes

destroyed (including Providence, Rhode Island), and some smaller tribes were nearly wiped out.

1682: Robert de La Salle claimed the Mississippi River Valley for the French empire.

1683: William Penn reached a truce with the North American Indians. First German immigrants reached North America. Roger Williams died.

1686: James II formed the Federation of New England with the intention of redesigning the administration of North America.

1688: At the birth of a male heir to James II, seven Whig lords began the Glorious Revolution when they invited William of Orange and Mary, James II's daughter, to claim the throne of England. James II subsequently fled to France.

1689: North American King William's War began as the English allied with the Iroquois. Iroquois Indians massacred French settlers at Lachine near Montreal.
Parliament proclaimed the abdication of James II which permitted the coronation of the Protestants William of Orange and Mary II. Parliament also passed the Act of Toleration for Trinitarian Protestants who were dissenters and the adopted the English Bill of Rights. John Locke anonymously published *Two Treatises on Government*, a blueprint of individual rights and limited government.

1690: The French settlement of Port Royal fell to the English. In Ireland, the Battle of Boyne resulted in James flight to the Continent.

1691: Plymouth Colony became a part of Massachusetts.

1692: William and Mary College founded in Virginia.

Insidious Changes

1700: Samuel Sewall published the first anti-slavery tract, "The Selling of Joseph."

1702: British forces attacked St. Augustine (Florida). Queen Anne ascended to the throne at the death of William III.

1704: During Queen Anne's War, French and Indian allies massacred the Puritans of Deerfield (Massachusetts).

1706: During Queen Anne's War, Charleston successfully withstood a siege of French and Spanish forces.

1707: In Queen Anne's War, British forces landed in Acadia. The Act of Union created Great Britain with the union of England and Scotland.

1710: In Queen Anne's War, the British under Francis Nicholson captured Port Royal (Annapolis Royal). However, future raids on Quebec and Montreal failed.

1712: Parliament enacted a Stamp Act.

1713: Peace of Utrecht ended the War of Spanish Succession and Queen Anne's War. Spain ceded Gibraltar and Minorca to Britain. Control of Newfoundland, Hudson Bay, and Acadia passed from France to Britain.

1718: Small pox inoculation introduced.

1721: Robert Walpole became the Prime Minister (recognized as the first) of King George I in Parliament.

1727: Quakers began formal opposition to slavery.

1729: Baltimore founded.

Insidious Changes

1732: Benjamin Franklin published "Poor Richard's Almanck" in Philadelphia.

1733: James Oglethorpe founded Savannah (Georgia). The Molasses Act prohibited British North American trade with the French West Indies.

1734: The charismatic minister Jonathan Edwards began the Great Awakening throughout the American colonies in a fifteen year religious revival that emphasized the relationship of the individual with God and de-emphasized formal church doctrine.

1735: John Peter Zenger, publisher of the "Weekly Journal" in New York, stood trial for seditious libel against the royal governor. In a landmark vote, the jury voted to acquit him, and therefore, established a principle of freedom of the press in America.

1739: The War of Jenkins' Ear, the prelude to the War of Austrian Succession in Europe, began after opponents of Robert Walpole's ministry invited Captain Robert Jenkins to testify of his loss of his ship *Rebecca* and his ear to the Spanish coast guard.

1745: In King George's War (War of Austrian Succession in Europe), British captured Louisbourg from the French.

1748: Peace of Aix-la-Chapelle ended the War of Austrian Succession (King George's War in North America). Britain regained control of Madras and returned Louisbourg to French control. This also ended the French-Indian and British-Iroquois raids in New England and New France.

1749: George Washington took an appointment as official surveyor of Culpeper County, Virginia.

1752: Britain adopted the Georgian calendar and eliminated 12 days in September.

1754: The French and Indian War began when George Washington (under orders from Virginia's lieutenant governor Robert Dinwiddie) attempted to build a fort at the confluence of the Allegheny and Monongahela rivers. The French had already erected Fort Duquesne. After building Fort Necessity in response to the French presence, Washington would be forced to surrender.

1755: General Braddock marched the British into an ambush and failed in his attack on Fort Duquesne: Washington averted a total massacre. This incident convinced Washington that the British officers suffered from arrogance.

1756: Britain joined Prussia against France, Austria, and Russia as the Seven Years' War began (an extension of the French and Indian War in North America).

1758: Louisbourg again fell to the British. The French Fort Duquesne fell to George Washington and John Forbes.

1759: Meeting the French in battle on the Plains of Abraham the British captured the city of Quebec. Both the French general Montcalm and British general James Wolfe died in the conflict.

1760: French forces failed to recapture Quebec and lost Montreal to the British. King George II died succeeded by his son George III.

1762: Britain established Maugerville in New Brunswick (the first British settlement in the area) and took control of Grenada and Havana in the Americas.

## REVOLUTION AND EARLY INDEPENDENCE

1763: The Treaty of Paris passed control of the St. Lawrence and Ohio River valleys from France to Britain as well as control of Florida from Spain to Britain. King George III issued the

Insidious Changes

Proclamation of 1763 (October) which prohibited English colonists from settling beyond the Appalachians.

1765: Parliament enacted the Stamp Act to provide for the payment of the defense of the American colonies.  The reaction resulted in the Stamp Act Congress and a declaration of rights and liberties.

1766: Stamp Act repealed.

1770: Import duties were repealed with the exception of tea.

1773: Boston Tea Party in protest of East India Company's monopoly of tea trade to America.

1774: Coercive (Intolerable) Acts passed in response to the Boston Tea Party.  First Continental Congress convened.

1775: American minutemen faced British regulars on the march toward Concord.  The shots of that April morning in Lexington began the American War of Independence.  The Second Continental Congress convened in May.  George Washington became the commanding general of the American forces.

1776: Thomas Paine published *Common Sense* in January.  In July, the Second Continental Congress issued the Declaration of Independence.  After several defeats and retreats during the Revolutionary War, Washington crossed the Delaware River on Christmas night and routed British forces twice.
In Britain, Adam Smith published his indictment of mercantilism in the *Wealth of Nations* which asserted that a government needs only to provide for the national defense, insure justice, and raise revenues for those undertakings that prove too costly for private investment.

1777: American forces defeated the British in the Battle of Saratoga, a victory that convinced the French and Spanish to support the American cause.  The Second Continental Congress drafted and

~ 184 ~

adopted the Articles of Confederation in November (the states ratified in March 1781).

1781: British forces surrendered at the Battle of Yorktown as the fighting ended in the American War of Independence

1783: The Peace of Paris extended the United States to the Mississippi River.

1786: Concerned with the lack of unity under the Articles of Confederation, several delegates met at Annapolis, Maryland. They adjourned without a plan other than to meet the following year.

## A CONSTITUTIONAL REPUBLIC

1787: In one of its most significant pieces of legislation under the Articles of Confederation, Congress set forth the procedures for the formation of states within the territory (Northwest Ordinance). However, the Philadelphia Convention, follow up to Annapolis, would draft a new constitution to be submitted to the states for ratification.

1789: In Paris, the Storming of the Bastille began the French Revolution.

1790: The Second Great Awakening began as a reaction to the Enlightenment. Self-improvement and social betterment led to social reforms including temperance, female equality, education and prison reform, and abolition. The Methodist and Baptist membership grew through numerous tent revivals. This Second Awakening lasted until 1840.
In Britain, Edmund Burke wrote his conservative political analysis entitled *Reflections on the Revolution in France.*

1791: In response to Burke, Thomas Paine wrote *The Rights of Man.* This radical interpretation of political rights resulted in Paine losing much of his former status as a defender of freedom in the American Revolutionary War.

1792: In Britain, Mary Wollstonecraft wrote *A Vindication of the Rights of Women*.

1793: In Georgia, Eli Whitney invented the cotton gin providing a boost to short staple cotton processed in the South and helped sustain a key industry supported by slavery.
King Louis XVI executed in France.

1798: After a build-up of tensions resulting from the Genêt Affair and France's hostile reaction to the Jay Treaty, the Federalists passed the Alien and Sedition Acts. These consisted of four acts; 1) the Naturalization Act extended the residency requirement for citizenship from five to fourteen years (directed against immigrants from the Continent), 2) the Alien Act allowed the president to expel dangerous aliens, 3) the Alien Enemies Act allowed the president to arrest, jail, and deport dangerous aliens during a time of war, and 4) the Sedition Act prohibited assembly to oppose the government and allowed press censorship. Thomas Jefferson and James Madison opposed these Federalist measures with the Kentucky and Virginia resolutions which declared the acts an assumption of power.

1799: Citing the unconstitutionality of the Alien and Sedition Acts, the second Kentucky resolution proposed that a state could "nullify" such legislation (this became a source of contention in the years leading to the Civil War).

1800: France purchased the territory of Louisiana from Spain. Washington, D.C. became the new capitol of the United States, and the Library of Congress opened. After a tie vote with Aaron Burr, the Electoral College selected Thomas Jefferson as president.

1801: Tripoli pirates began the Barbary War against American shipping for US refusal to pay tribute.

~ 186 ~

1803: The United States purchased Louisiana from the French for $15 million (sixty million francs, $0.04 an acre). Supreme Court Chief Justice John Marshall established the principle of judicial review of Congressional acts in the case *Marbury v. Madison*.

1804: Meriwether Lewis and William Clark left St. Louis to explore the Louisiana Territory.

1805: The Barbary War between Tripoli pirates and the United States ended.

1807: St. Louis entrepreneur Manuel Lewis established a trading post at Little Big Horn, a fort which opened the west to fur trapping with an influx of "mountain men." Robert Fulton and Robert Livingston launched the steamship *Clermont* which journeyed from New York to Albany on the Hudson River and revolutionized transportation.

1812: Although Britain agreed to cease impressing American sailors into His Majesty's Service on June 16, the U.S. declared war on June 19 (with an eye on Florida which was under Spanish control). Detroit fell to British troops.

1813: Tecumseh died in battle and along with him the tribal federation he led against the US.

1814: British troops burned Washington, DC, but Dolley Madison had the presence of mind to grab the portrait of George Washington as the presidential family fled the White House. Battle of Plattsburgh secured the northern American border. After an all night siege of Fort McHenry outside Baltimore, Francis Scott Key saw the American flag flying the next morning and penned the poem, "The Defence of Fort McHenry." Eventually it was put to music and the tune named the "Star-Spangled Banner" which officially became the national anthem in 1931. In the Battle of New Orleans Andrew Jackson turned back the British.

Insidious Changes

1815: The War of 1812 ended. In Europe, Wellington and von Blucher defeated Napoleon for the final time at the Battle of Waterloo.

1817: Construction of the Erie Canal began.

1819: Panic of 1819 sent the economy into a tailspin. In a case supporting Congressional power through the elastic clause, the Supreme Court upheld the position of the Second Bank of the United States in *McCulloch v. Maryland*. The Senate ratified the Adams-Onis Treaty with Spain which established the border of Mexico.

## THE ROAD TO CIVIL WAR

1820: Maine joined the union as a free state under the Missouri Compromise (had been a part of Massachusetts). After Missouri's admission, slavery would be prohibited above its southern border.

1821: Missouri became a state.

1823: In response to Russian claims in the Pacific Northwest, the US issued the Monroe Doctrine and Great Britain supported the policy.

1830: Congress passed the Indian Removal Act beginning a movement of the Five Civilized Tribes from the Southeast to the West. The force migration will gain the title of "The Trail of Tears." Joseph Smith published *The Book of Mormon*.

1831: Nat Turner rebellion in southern Virginia resulted in a slave uprising that left about 65 dead. Turner hid out for several weeks before being captured, tried and hung. As a result of the rebellion, laws enforcing slavery became much harsher.

1832: Dissatisfied with high Western land prices, anti-slavery sentiment, and a high tariff passed by Congress, the South Carolina

~ 188 ~

legislature passed the Ordinance of Nullification which proposed to disregard the new tariff. Andrew Jackson issued the "Proclamation to the People of South Carolina" which expressed his determination to maintain the union. South Carolina delayed the enforcement of their ordinance, and in March 1833 Congress passed a reduced tariff.

1834: Cyrus McCormick patented his reaper and John Deere developed a workable steel plow opening the heavy soil of the Midwest to increased farming.
Imperial slavery outlawed by the British Parliament.

1836: Santa Anna laid siege and took the Alamo in Texas killing all of the rebels who had taken a defensive position within the old mission.

1839: Violence erupted with the British over Maine's border with Canada.

1840: After traveling much of the US, Alexis de Tocqueville completed his publication, *Democracy in America* describing the American culture of self-government.

1842: The Webster-Ashburton Treaty settled the boundary of Canada and Maine.

1844: On May 24, Samuel Morse transmitted a telegraphic message from Washington, DC to Baltimore. Telegraph lines would soon provide communication throughout the US.

1845: Frederick Douglass, an escaped slave, published *Narrative of the Life of Frederick Douglass* which launched his leadership as an antislavery leader. In February, Congress passed an act to annex Texas which the Republic of Texas approved in June. John O'Sullivan, editor of the New York *Post*, first used the term "manifest destiny." Potato famine in Ireland would begin a massive movement from the Emerald Island to North America.

1846: The Oregon Treaty established with the 49th Parallel as boundary in the northwest between U.S. and British North America. May 13, the U.S. declared war on Mexico. The Bear Flag Revolt erupted in California under John C. Fremont and William Ide, and ended with the California Republic proclaiming to be a part of the US.

1847: The Mormons began their mass migration to present-day Utah.

1848: Treaty of Guadalupe Hidalgo ended the Mexican American War. First gold found at Sutter's Mill in California.

1849: California Gold Rush began its peak period.

1850:   Britain agreed to be less active in Central America through the Clayton-Bulwer Treaty.

1852: Harriet Beecher Stowe published *Uncle Tom's Cabin*. The California Gold Rush peak ended.

1853: Commodore Matthew Perry made his first visit to Japan.

1854: Congress passed the Kansas-Nebraska Act allowing new states to accept slavery by popular vote. Commodore Perry made his second visit to Japan resulting in relations between the US and Japan.

1856: As American politics fractured, Democrat James Buchanan handily won the presidency.

1857: The Dred Scott decision stated that slaves had no citizenship rights.

1859: Edwin Drake and William Smith struck oil in Titusville, Pennsylvania. John Brown led a raid on Harpers Ferry as a protest to slavery.

Insidious Changes

1860: Pony Express began operation. Republican Abraham Lincoln elected president without winning a single Southern state.

1861: On April 12, shots rang out at Fort Sumter and the American Civil War began.

1862: Congress passed the Homestead Act.

1863: President Lincoln issued the Emancipation Proclamation.

1865: The states ratified the 13th Amendment ending slavery in the U.S. The American Civil War officially ended.

1866: The first organization of the Ku Klux Klan and Black Codes restricting the civil liberties of former slaves appeared in Tennessee. Charlie Goodnight and Oliver Loving blazed a cattle drive from Texas to Colorado. Indian Wars began in the West.

1868: Ratification of the 14th Amendment established due process and equality under the law in states guaranteed by the federal government.

1869: In May, the Union Pacific and the Central Pacific met at Promontory Point, Utah and drove the "golden" Last Spike to complete the First Transcontinental Railroad. The Wyoming territory provided women with the right to vote.

1870: Ratification of the 15th Amendment gave black males the vote. John D. Rockefeller founded Standard Oil.

1872: US granted a large sum of damages from Britain for the destruction caused by the British built ship *Alabama* used by the Confederates.

1873: Financial panic in Europe spread to US as foreign capital was withdrawn from the American economy worsening the recession.

1876: Centennial of the US. Just a few days before the national celebration, General George Custer and his unit were wiped out in the

Insidious Changes

Battle of Little Big Horn by Lakota, Northern Cheyenne, and Arapaho forces. Alexander Graham Bell patented the telephone.

1877: With the Congressional arrangement ending the contested presidential election of 1876, Reconstruction ended in the South and Rutherford B. Hayes became president.

## INDUSTRIAL AMERICA

1879: Thomas Edison invented the electric light bulb.

1881: Booker T. Washington founded the Tuskegee Institute. Clara Barton founded the American Red Cross.

1884: France donated the Statue of Liberty to the US.

1889: Oklahoma Land Rush. Panama Canal construction stalled because of a lack of funding.

1890: The Progressive Era began. Congress passed the Sherman Antitrust Act. The last major battle of the Indian Wars ended at Wounded Knee with a massacre of hundreds of Lakota Indians, about half being women and children. Wyoming granted statehood.

1893: The British divested American loans resulting in a bank panic. Colorado gives women the right to vote.

1895: Guglielmo Marconi invented wireless telegraphy leading to radio and television in the 20th Century.

1896: Klondike gold rush began. Alfred Nobel died and the Nobel prizes were founded. Modern Olympic Games began in Athens. Women gained the right to vote in Idaho and Utah.

1899: Secretary of State John Hay issued the "Open Door" policy allowing for accessible trade with China. The ensuing treaty between the US, Japan, and many European countries lasted until the regime of Mao Zedong 50 years later.

1900: Boxer Rebellion in China; Europeans besieged in Peking.

1901: Boxer Rebellion in China was suppressed. Panamanian revolt opened the door for US construction of the Panama Canal. Marconi transmitted a wireless message across the Atlantic Ocean.

1903: Orville and Wilbur Wright made their first successful flight at Kitty Hawk. The film "The Great Train Robbery" debuted.

1904: Senate ratified the Panama Canal Treaty.

1905: William "Big Bill" Haywood founded the Industrial Workers of the World organization, or the Wobblies, envisioning one large industrial union in the US.

1907: Panic of 1907 caused economic turmoil.

1908: Henry Ford introduced the Model T.

1909: The National Association for the Advancement of Colored People formed.

1911: Congress passed the Federal Reserve Act creating a national bank in the US.

1912: Robert La Follette founded the Progressive Party. Theodore Roosevelt joined and ran as the Bull Moose candidate effectively splitting the Republican vote and handing the presidency to Woodrow Wilson.

1913: The ratification of the Sixteenth Amendment granted the federal government the right to collect income taxes. The Federal Reserve System began operation.

1914: The assassination of Archduke Ferdinand of Austria led to World War I.

1915: The sinking of the *Lusitania* resulted in the death of 128 Americans from a German U-boat attack.

Congress adopted the American Creed celebrating liberty, equality, individualism, accountability, and free markets.

1917: After the Zimmerman Telegraph in January and the German declaration of unrestricted U-boat warfare on commercial shipping, the US declared war on the Central Powers (April).
The October Revolution broke open in Russia. Under the Treaty of Brest-Livtosk, Russian forces left the war.

1918: Decisive Second Battle of Marne turned back the Germans and proved to be a turning point in the war. On November 11, armistice ended the war leaving German troops on foreign soil, leading to the myth of treason during the Weimar Republic.
The Spanish Flu pandemic hit infecting about a third of the global population.

1919: Red Scare in the US. Treaty of Versailles established the conditions of peace in Europe.

1920: The Progressive Era ended.
League of Nations founded (the US would be an observer, but never fully joined the body).

1922: The Union of Soviet Socialist Republics formed as the Russian Civil War ended with a Bolshevik victory.

1925: Soviet founder Lenin died.

1927: Charles Lindbergh crossed the Atlantic Ocean in the "Spirit of St. Louis." Anarchists Sacco and Vanzetti were executed for murder. Germany fell into a financial crisis. Josef Stalin took control of the Soviet Union and his rival Trotsky fled the country (to be murdered in Mexico in 1940).

1929: Black Friday (October 29) marked the beginning of the Great Depression: it spread to be global.

1930: Smoot-Hawley Tariff passed helping to cause an even deeper economic depression.

Insidious Changes

1931: Congress adopted the "Star-Spangled Banner" as the National Anthem.
The Manchurian Incident (Japanese invasion of Korea) failed to provoke a response from the League of Nations.

## NEW DEAL AMERICA

1932: Ottawa Conference instituted protective tariffs for Commonwealth trading partners.

1933: In Germany, President Hindenburg asked Adolf Hitler, who headed the largest party (although still a minority) of the Reichstag, to assume the Chancellorship and form a government.

1934: The Reichstag gave Hitler dictatorial powers. Stalin began his army leadership purge in the Soviet Union.

1936: The Spanish Civil War began: a testing ground for the forces of Hitler and Stalin. FDR unveiled his Court Packing Plan.

1937: Neville Chamberlain became the British Conservative Prime Minister. The Supreme Court's Switch in Time that Saved Nine ended the Court Packing controversy with FDR.

1938: Czechoslovakia given to Germany at the Munich Conference.

1939: Francisco Franco gained control of Spain as the civil war ended with the surrender of Madrid. On September 1, Germany and the USSR, by mutual agreement, invaded Poland to begin World War II. The Declaration of Panama stated prohibition of belligerent activity in waters of the Americas south of Canada (300 mile range provided basis for FDR's patrolling for German U-boats).

## WORLD WAR II

1941: The Lend-Lease Program passed Congress allowing some material support of the Allies. With persistence from FDR, the Americans and British issued the Atlantic Charter. December 7 the

Insidious Changes

Japanese held a dawn raid on the American naval base Pearl Harbor, Hawaii. The next day the US officially entered World War II.

1942: The Battle of the Coral Sea, Midway, and Guadalcanal all contributed to rolling back Japanese expansion. German U-boats continued to sink American ships in the North Atlantic, but Germany lost men, materials, and territory in Stalingrad and North Africa. The War Production Board went into full gear overseeing manufacturing production, freezing prices and wages as taxes were increased: the rationing of gasoline also ensued. FDR issued Executive Order 9066 authorizing internment of those of Japanese descent.

1943: At the Casablanca Conference, the Allies set forth the terms of ending the war: unconditional surrender. In February, the last Germans surrendered at Stalingrad. Germans and Italians surrendered at Tunisia: Allies gained control of the Mediterranean. The Allies landed on Sicily in July, Mussolini resigned, and the Allies landed on the Italian peninsula in September. Although the Italian government would officially surrender, Germany would fight the Allies in the rugged mountains of the peninsula. Churchill and FDR planned a Pacific strategy in Cairo (with Chinese nationalist Chiang Kai-shek). In Tehran, the two met with Stalin to plan an invasion of Europe from the north.

1944: On June 6, the Allies launched a massive invasion of Normandy in northern France. The Germans were put on the defensive, launching their last attempt at an offensive with the Battle of the Bulge in December.
In the Pacific theater, the Allies gained a big victory in June in the Battle of the Philippine Sea. Kamikaze pilots were pressed into action, but the Japanese continued to lose. They suffered another crushing blow in the Battle of Leyte Gulf (October 25, the largest one-day naval battle in history).
Back home, the Bretton Woods Conference in July provided a framework for the postwar financial system with the establishment of the International Monetary Fund and the World Bank. In November, FDR handily won reelection with his new vice-president Harry Truman of Missouri.

~ 196 ~

As the war wound down, FDR believed he could continue to work with Stalin in a cooperative manner. Truman, on the other hand, became increasingly suspicious of the Soviet leader. As a result of the growing tension, Truman's administration set the stage for the next 45 years of American foreign policy, containment of the Soviet Union became the enduring strategy of the Cold War.

1945: April 12, FDR died and Truman became president. May 8, Germany surrendered, and the Allies declared VE Day. Americans, British, French, and Soviets divided Germany into occupation zones at Potsdam. On August 6, the US dropped an atomic bomb on Hiroshima, Japan, and August 9 dropped a second on Nagasaki, Japan. On August 14, the Allies declared VJ Day (Japan formally signed surrender aboard USS *Missouri* on September 2). On October 24, 51 countries formed the United Nations organization. Vietnam became independent of French Indochina with Ho Chi Minh as the first president.

## THE COLD WAR

1946: The UN General Assembly and Security Council convened in London and New York. Winston Churchill gave his "Iron Curtain" speech at Westminster College in Fulton, Missouri.
Congress passed the Employment Security Act implying major responsibility for controlling the business cycle and creating the Council of Economic Advisers.

1947: In the Everson decision, the Supreme Court used the Jeffersonian phrase "wall of separation" (from his 1802 letter to the Danbury Baptists reassuring them that the government would not interfere with religion) to describe the relationship of government and religion.

1949: China fell to Mao Zedong as Chiang Kai-shek fled with Nationalist forces to the island of Formosa (Taiwan). North Atlantic Treaty Organization (NATO) formed.

1950: Senator Joseph McCarthy began an investigation of Communists in the US. North Korean troops invaded South Korea.

Insidious Changes

UN troops held out at Pusan and counter attacked through Inchon Bay. Chinese troops invaded North Korea, Chinese also invaded Tibet

1951: Truman dismissed MacArthur as UN commander in Korea. Truce talks began. Truman dispatched federal troops in railroad strike.

1952: Dwight D. Eisenhower, former Supreme Allied Commander in Europe, ran as Republican candidate for President winning in a landslide.

1953: Julius and Ethel Rosenberg were executed for passing atomic secrets to the Soviets. Joseph Stalin died. Korean cease fire signed. The US and South Korea signed a mutual defense treaty.

1954: The Warren Court heard *Brown v. Board of Education* and subsequently ended segregation with its decision that separate is inherently unequal. French troops at Dien Bien Phu surrendered. Vietnam divided by treaty at 17th parallel, Ho Chi Minh ruled the north and Ngo Dinh Diem ruled in the south. Full elections promised in two years (never held). Laos and Cambodia were given independence.
US and Japan signed mutual defense treaty. USSR rejects western proposal to unify Germany, occupation of West Germany ended. US Senate formally condemned Joseph McCarthy's hearings.

1955: With defiance from Rosa Parks, the Montgomery Bus boycott began.
South Vietnam became a republic. Indian Health Service established for recognized Native American tribe members. UN accepted universal membership principle (allowed 14 previously excluded nations to join).

1956: Congress passed the Interstate Highway Act which became the largest public works project in history. Hungary withdrew from Warsaw Pact, and Soviets responded with a tank invasion. UN condemned Soviets but took no action.

Congress adopted "In God We Trust" as the official national motto replacing the unofficial motto of *"E pluribus unum"* (Out of many, one) used since the Revolution.

1957: USSR launched *Sputnik* placing a satellite in orbit. Belgium, France, West Germany, Italy, Luxembourg, and the Netherlands signed the Treaty of Rome to establish the European Economic Community.

1958: French Fourth Republic fell: Charles de Gaulle recalled from retirement to form a new government which became the Fifth Republic. US launched *Explorer* 1 satellite.

1959: Alaska (49) and Hawaii (50) admitted as states.

1960: John F. Kennedy elected president.

1962: In a speech at Rice University, JFK called for the US to put a man on the moon before the end of the decade.

1963: Betty Friedan published *The Feminine Mystique* in the US providing a focal point for the American feminist movement. In October, JFK was assassinated in Dallas: Lee Harvey Oswald arrested as the shooter, but shot by Jack Ruby before facing trial.

1964: Congress passed the Civil Rights Act and the Tonkin Gulf Resolution which permitted Lyndon Johnson to escalate the War in Vietnam. Johnson called for a "War on Poverty," Equal Employment Opportunity Act passed. Supreme Court ruled that the 14th Amendment provided for the "one man, one vote" principle.

1965: Medicare established as health care for elderly Americans, Medicaid established for those of lower income.

1966: Supreme Court ruled in *Miranda v. State of Arizona* requiring the accused criminals understand their rights when they are arrested. Betty Friedan formed the National Organization of Women (NOW).

1967: US, USSR and UK signed treaty forbidding use of nuclear weapons in space. US *Apollo* 3 exploded on launch pad killing all three astronauts. The Six Day War erupted and ended in Middle East.

1968: USS *Pueblo* seized by the North Vietnamese. US planes bombed North Vietnamese trails into the south and Vietcong bases in Laos and Cambodia. Tet Offensive opened by the North Vietnamese. Martin Luther King, Jr. and Robert Kennedy assassinated. Richard Nixon elected President.
The US, USSR, UK and 58 other nations signed a nuclear non-proliferation pact. Alexander Dubcek became Communist leader in Czechoslovakia, he eased political restrictions and granted freedom of the press, but Soviet tank units invaded Prague and forcefully installed a hard-line Communist regime.

1969: American Astronaut Neil Armstrong became first human to walk on the moon.

1970: The US and South Vietnamese invaded Cambodia to destroy Vietcong bases and troops. Nixon announced that 150,000 American troops would be withdrawn from South Vietnam in the following year (some drawdown had begun in 1969). Four students were killed by National Guardsmen at Kent State University.
Communist Salvador Allende became president of Chile and sought closer ties to Communist nations. Allende announced plans to nationalize foreign banks and companies. China launched its first satellite.

1971: The New York *Times* published the "Pentagon Papers" (MIT Professor Daniel Ellsberg leaked *The History of the U.S. Decision Making Process in Vietnam* to reporter Neil Sheehan). *US v New York Times*. The US suspended conversion of dollars into gold. South Vietnamese troops invaded Laos; North Vietnamese captured the Plains of Jars. Communist China admitted to UN; Taiwan withdrew. Three Cosmonauts killed when their space capsule lost air pressure on earth landing.

1972: The US and USSR agreed to end arms race with the Strategic Arms Limitation Talks (SALT I), US bombed Hanoi and Hiaphon and blockaded North Vietnamese ports. Supreme Court ruling suspended death penalty. Nixon reelected by a landslide

1973: The Watergate break-in became public: John Erlichman and H. R. Haldeman resigned. Spiro Agnew resigned as Vice President of US under tax evasion scandal, Gerald Ford chosen as successor. Supreme Court legalized abortion in *Roe v. Wade*.
Oil crises caused further financial strain in US; dollar devalued by 10percent. Libya took 51percent control of US oil companies in that nation. Egyptians and Syrians attacked Israelis, Egypt regained part of Sinai, Arab oil producers imposed an embargo and crude prices doubled.
During an army coup, Chilean President Allende committed suicide.

1974: After continued congressional investigations and drawing up of Article of Impeachment in the House, Nixon resigned succeeded by Gerald Ford. Ford appointed Nelson Rockefeller Vice President of US. Ford pardoned Nixon.

1975: US troops left Cambodia. In April, South Vietnam fell to North Vietnam (unconditional surrender). A federal loan saved New York City from bankruptcy. Supreme Court ruling ended union "closed shops".
Britain reaffirmed Common Market membership; British referendum reaffirmed Common Market in EEC.

1976: Chinese leadership changed when Premier Chou En-lai died. Teng Hsia-ping was dismissed, and Mao Zedong died. Hua Kuo-feng rose to power and Mao's widow, Chiang Ching, along with other radical leaders were purged by regime of Deng Xiaoping.
Democrat Jimmy Carter elected president. Vietnam was officially reunited.

1977: The *Concorde* (supersonic passenger jet) won rights to land at New York's Kennedy Airport.
Eleven oil exporting nations raised prices 15percent. Oil began to flow through Alaska Pipeline.

1978: Chinese encouraged foreign study and foreign investment in new modernization policy. Vietnam invaded Cambodia and installed a favorable regime. Under a treaty US retained control of Panama Canal. Unrest against Nicaraguan dictator Anastasio Somoza began (he would leave the country a year later).
Menachem Begin and Anwar Sadat attended peace talks at Camp David. Cubans began a more active role in Angola civil war.
Alexander Solzhenitsyn's *Gulag Archipelago* published exposing the forced labor camps for the political prisoners of the Soviet Union.
Pope Paul VI died and his successor John Paul I died suddenly to be succeeded by John Paul II, a Polish cardinal.

1979: The US and China reestablished diplomatic relations while separate US relations were retained with Taiwan. Three Mile Island nuclear plant accident resulted in no casualties. The US and Soviet Union signed the SALT II treaty (not ratified in the US Senate). The Shah of Iran left Iran in the wake of revolution. Islamic revolutionaries took control of the American embassy in Tehran, Iran and held American personnel as captives. The second oil shock helped to raise American inflation to its highest level since the Great Depression.
Margaret Thatcher became the Conservative Prime Minister of Britain and would form a tight bond with Ronald Reagan.

1980: Americans disguised as Canadians escaped captivity in Tehran. An American helicopter rescue mission failed after crashing. The USSR invaded Afghanistan to support its Communist regime. The US placed a grain and high technical embargo on the Soviets, and boycotted Moscow Olympics. Ronald Reagan elected president.

1981: During President Reagan's inauguration, Iranian revolutionaries released the American hostages. The US lifted its grain embargo against the USSR.
Poland declared martial law against union dissidents. El Salvador began receiving US military advisors. Chinese "Gang of Four" tried and convicted of abuses that occurred during the Cultural Revolution.

1982: Falklands War broke out between Argentina and Britain. Britain retained the islands.

~ 202 ~

1983: Oil prices dropped. Soviet fighter shot down a Korean airliner and killed 269 passengers. US marines joined a UN peacekeeping force in Beirut, Lebanon and 240 died in a suicide attack from Muslim terrorists. In alliance with Caribbean nations, the US invaded Grenada and expelled a Cuban troop presence. Reagan gave public support to the Strategic Defense Initiative (SDI). US cruise missiles installed in Britain.

1984: Britain agreed to return Hong Kong to Chinese control in 1997. During economic recovery the US dollar rose sharply against foreign currencies.
Reagan visited China. Soviet bloc nations boycotted Los Angeles Olympics.

1985: New Soviet Premier Mikhail Gorbachev held first meeting with Reagan in Geneva.

1986: After an attack on American Marines in a West Berlin nightclub, the US froze Libyan financial assets in its borders. The US bombed Benghazi and Tripoli in retaliation. The Iran-Contra affair became public. US-USSR disarmament talks stalled over the Strategic Defense Initiative.

1987: Reagan White House Chief of Staff Donald Regan resigned over Tower Commission Report concerning the Iran-Contra Affair. Congressional hearings began on the subject. October 19, Black Monday, Dow Jones Industrial Average dropped 508.32 points losing 22percent of its value: several safeguards subsequently came into use in an attempt to modify the exacerbating affect of high-frequency trading (HFT).
The US and USSR agreed to reduce number of medium-range nuclear missiles in Europe.

1988: US Congress refused aid to Contra rebels in Nicaragua. US opposition to Manuel Noriega precipitated an economic crisis in Panama.
A terrorist bomb killed 259 Pan Am airline passengers during a crash at Lockerbie, Scotland.

Iranians mined the Persian Gulf; US navy destroyed two Iranian oil platforms and thwarted a counterattack; USS *Vincennes* accidentally shot down an Iranian passenger plane resulting in 290 deaths.
Tiananmen Square crackdown in China scattered protestors seeking more open government in the PRC.
George H. W. Bush elected president.

1989: Vietnamese troops withdrew from Cambodia. US supported coup in Panama failed; Noriega declared a state of war and US invaded the country and captured Noriega.
By October, British computer scientist Tim Berners-Lee had developed three underlying technologies of the World Wide Web allowing different computers to communicate more smoothly. These were: Hypertext Markup Language (HTML), Uniform Resource Identifier (URI), and Hypertext Transfer Protocol (HTTP). He also developed the first web browser.
The USSR began to unravel. Bush visited Hungary and Poland and offered financial aid; "Velvet Revolution" challenged Soviets in Czechoslovakia; the Berlin Wall fell in December.

1990: US agreed to economic aid to USSR and granted the Soviets most-favored-nation trading status, and MFN restored to China. Iraq invaded Kuwait and US and USSR denounced the move. US and Allied troops moved into Saudi Arabia in the protective maneuver named Operation Desert Shield. John Major replaced Margaret Thatcher as the British Conservative Prime Minister.

1991: Congress authorized the Al Gore-sponsored High Performance Computing Act to help develop an open internet: Mosaic web browser would be developed within the National Information Infrastructure (which Gore nicknamed the Information Highway, harkening back to one of President Reagan's favored phrases).
Desert Storm forced Iraq to sue for peace in four days. No fly zones would be established.
A Soviet coup attempt of August failed and gave rise to Russian president Boris Yeltsin. In December, the USSR collapsed and the Cold War ended when Gorbachev resigned and handed the Soviet nuclear launch codes to Yeltsin.

# THE POST COLD WAR WORLD

1992: Alabama became the 38th state to ratify the 27th Amendment. Democrat Bill Clinton won the presidential election.

1993: Terrorists set off bomb in garage underneath the World Trade Center in New York. "Don't ask, don't tell" policy adopted for gay military members. Clinton signed North American Free Trade Agreement into law to be effective less than a month later on January 1.
The Hawaii Supreme Court called for trial to demonstrate if traditional marriage furthered the interest of the state.
The Internet became commercialized launching the Internet, Dotcom boom.

1995: In the worst domestic terrorist attack in American history, a truck bomb killed 168 people in Oklahoma City. Timothy McVeigh and Terry Nichols were convicted of the crime: McVeigh would be put to death in 2001 and Nichols received several life sentences.

1996: Terrorist bombing of Khobar Towers in Saudi Arabia left 19 American soldiers dead. Bomb at Centennial Park in Atlanta during Summer Olympic Games kills one and injures 111. Clinton reelected president.
Congress passed and Clinton signed the Defense of Marriage Act defining marriage as between a man and a woman under federal law as well as welfare reform.

1998: House impeached Clinton surrounding affair with intern Monica Lewinsky.
Hawaii voters passed constitutional amendment allowing state legislature to ban same-sex marriages; Alaskans passed constitutional amendment banning same-sex marriages.

1999: Senate acquited Clinton on impeachment charges. The Dow Jones Industrial Average broke 10,000.

2000: Despite angst and a lot of recoding, the Y2K bug did not appear at the turn of the year, and the Dotcom boom started to unravel. George W. Bush elected president.

2001: Terrorists attacked the World Trade Towers on 9/11. US forces invaded Afghanistan in Operation Enduring Freedom. The USA PATRIOT Act passed to track terrorist activity within the US.

2003: Operation Iraqi Freedom removes Saddam Hussein from power.
In *Lawrence v. Texas*, the US Supreme Court struck down same-sex sodomy laws. Massachusetts Supreme Court rules that state constitution requires same-sex marriage to be legally recognized.

2004: In reaction to the Court's Lawrence decision, states began adopting measures in favor of traditional marriage.
Facebook officially launched.
George W. Bush reelected president.

2006: Democrats reclaimed both chambers of Congress.

2008: Global financial collapse hit. Barack Obama elected president.

2009: Tea Parties began to form calling for smaller government, fiscal restraint, individual freedom, and conservative interpretations of the Constitution as Congress passed large economic stimulus package. Iowa Supreme Court overturns traditional marriage statute as violation of equal protection clause of state constitution. Vermont became first state to legislatively approve same-sex marriage.

2010: Congress passed Obamacare. Republicans retook House and reduced Democrat Senate majority in November elections.
In popular votes, 28 of 30 statutes favoring traditional marriage had been adopted by states.

2011: Osama bin Laden killed in Pakistan by American forces.

2012: Obama reelected president.

2013: Supreme Court struck down the Defense of Marriage Act resulting in the federal government recognizing same-sex marriages (*US v. Windsor*).

2015: *Obergefell v. Hodges* legalized same-sex marriage throughout the US.

2016: In *Evenwel v. Abbot* the Supreme Court decided that the 14th Amendment allows states to allocate representatives based on population rather than voting-eligible population. Republican Donald Trump elected president.

2019: Democrat controlled House approved two Articles of Impeachment against President Trump, but Senate acquitted.

2020: The COVID-19 virus caused shutdowns across the US and in many other countries.